Dedication

This guide is dedicated to master harp player Cary Bell who died on May 6th, 2007 at the age of 70. Cary was one of my influences growing up. As a teenager I listened to his smooth, effortless playing on The London Muddy Waters Sessions album, floored by his warm tone and perfect vibrato.

Once I started to write "The Talking Harmonica", I thought about adding a photo that would speak to the concept of the book. I remembered one of my favorite photos, of Cary and me taken performing together at a blues festival in Salem, Massachusetts. What makes it perfect for this guide is that you can see Cary talking to me through his harp playing and myself hanging on his every word.

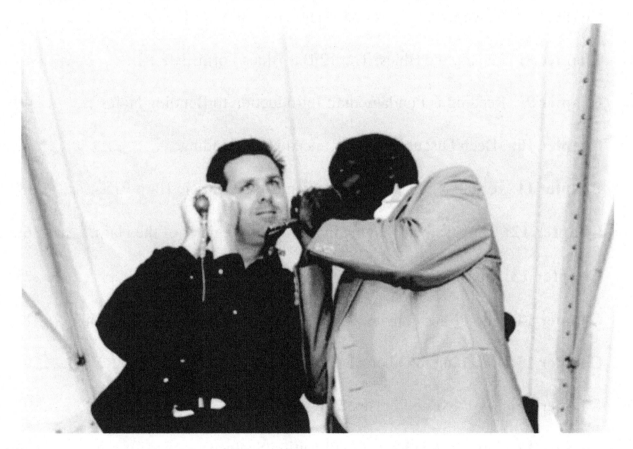

Chapters

Acknowledgements

I would like to thank the following for their advice, input and support: Kristen Dubee, Sherry Harris, Brad Nail, Mark England, Brian Gartland, Bill Gartland, Pat Gartland, Maureen Gartland, Mick Rogers, David Dumas, and Charles Sawyer.

Also, I would like to extend a very special thank you to the wonderful musicians that made the companion music for this book, Wilson Brown on drums, Paul Justice on bass and guitar, Ted Armstrong on piano. Joe Giardella added guitar on Chapter 22 and Tim Gartland added guitar on chapters 27 and 32.

Jim Saley took the photo of Cary and I. Wilson Brown, Trish Gartland and Scott Burk took all other photos.

The drawing of Little Walter in Chapter 15 is by Dennis Kempel.

To all my students, you have taught me so much…

Finally, very special thanks to Patricia Gartland for her advice, support and for living with me during the process of writing this guide.

Tim Gartland plays Seydel Harmonicas.

Please visit us at www.timgartland.com.

Salutation

To the earliest generations of players...
You transformed the harmonica beyond its humble designs to the
sophisticated instrument it is today.
-Tim Gartland

Chapter 1

First Words: How to Use this Guide

"Faith is taking the first step even when you don't see the whole staircase."

- Martin Luther King

Playing the harmonica (a.k.a the harp) is a lot like learning to talk. To talk, you need to learn words and sentences, as well as develop a sound to your voice. To play the harmonica, you need to learn how to play notes, scales and develop your sound.

You can't see how people talk and you can't see how people play harmonica. Both are learned through listening to others and learning how to imitate what you hear. In addition, just like learning to talk, you will use vowel and consonant sounds to help you speak the language of the harmonica.

The Talking Harmonica guide provides written lessons on how to speak the language of the harp. **The companion MP3's that can be downloaded for free at www.timgartland.com will let you hear the music as it is written in the guide.** Some people are more visual, some are more auditory; combining the guide with the MP3's gives you the best of both worlds. The written guide will show you the notes to play and the MP3's will allow you to listen to how they are played.

I have also included **You Tube** demonstrations. These demonstrations will be for techniques where learning is enhanced through visual demonstration.

The guide will focus on how to perform an exercise or song. It will describe the techniques and walk you through how to do it. The songs in the guide are written in an easy to follow format and include all the notes needed to perform them. The guide will refer you to the track on the MP3's where you can hear the music performed. Here you will learn the timing or phrasing of the song.

The MP3's will focus almost entirely on performing the music in the chapter. The first time through the demonstration, we will take it in "slo-go-motion" so you can easily follow the lesson. We will then speed up the exercise for you to hear what it will sound like in real speed.

How long until you can play? If you practice daily using this guide, after 30 days you will able to play songs and can call yourself a harmonica player.

Who is this guide for?

Aspiring Harmonica Heroes:

This guide will work for you if this is your first time picking up the harmonica or if you already play and want to accelerate your progress.

Musicians who play other instruments and are looking to add the harp to their musical arsenal:

You've got a leg up. You know the effort it takes to learn an instrument. There are a couple of sections that cover music theory, which you are probably already familiar with. Feel free to fast-forward through those sections.

How much time do I need to commit to this?

Everyone is busy these days. We all have to manage our time wisely. The ideal amount of practice time would be several short sessions a day, 10 to 15 minutes in length. However you do it, try to play daily, even if it is only for 5 minutes.

What is the best way to practice?

We all tend to play things that we already can play well. The key to getting better is working on the things we struggle with. If you find yourself struggling with a song or an exercise, identify the parts you are having trouble with. Take that section, isolate it and focus on playing only that section until you can play it smoothly. Then go back to playing the entire piece.

Private Lessons?

I do in person lessons. I have a teaching studio. I also give lessons via Skype to students around the world. Email me at: tim@timgartland.com.

Demonstration: Track 1 on MP3's, visit www.timgartland.com: Introduction

Chapter 2

Finding Your Voice:
Finding, Holding and Caring

"Creativity is not the finding of a thing, but the making
something out of it after it is found."

- James Russell Lowell

The first step in playing an instrument is finding one. The next steps are learning how to hold and care for it. This guide is designed for playing the *diatonic harmonica*, which is also commonly referred to as the *mouth harp* or just *harp*. The diatonic harp is the small harmonica you most commonly hear in contemporary music. It is the choice of such artists as Bob Dylan, Kim Wilson, Mick Jagger and Charlie Musselwhite.

Isn't a harp an elegant stringed instrument played by a glamorous young woman? Could be, but here we will refer to the diatonic harmonica as a harp. Early African-American players labeled it "the harp".

The harp is designed to play the seven major notes in the major scale (the white keys on the piano when playing the C major scale) and chords that are made from the scale. However, as we will learn, through the imaginations of artists with humble means but loads of talent, they discovered how to play the chromatic notes, the black keys if you will, and more...much more.

Here are some vital stats on the harp:

* It's the only instrument that can make music by blowing out and drawing in air.

* They are inexpensive, although they do go out of tune and need to be replaced.

* It has ten holes that are numbered 1 to 10.

* It is a reed instrument with the sound created by moving air over a metal reed.

* The longer the reed, the lower the note. The number 1 hole has the lowest notes; number ten has the highest notes.

* Between the top cover plates are the reed plates and the comb.

* The combs are typically made of plastic, aluminum or wood.

* Plastic combs do not warp and are easier to play.

✻ Wood combs have a warmer sound quality or tone.

✻ Harps come in all twelve keys of music.

✻ Harp players switch harps when songs are in different keys.

Different keys of the harmonica sound and play differently because they have higher or lower degrees of pitch. The key of G is the lowest, F# is the highest. This sound difference is demonstrated on track 2 on the MP3's.

****SPOTLIGHT****

For beginners, I recommend the modern harmonicas with plastic combs. The holes tend to be larger making it simpler to play single notes. Also, the reeds are easier to bend than older models. For this guide you will need to start with a harp in the key of C. Later, you will want to pick up one in the key of A.

Harp Holding

This section will teach you the classic style of holding the harp. How you hold it has an impact on your playing. It is the same as proper hand positioning in playing the guitar, piano, or other wind instruments.

The harp is held primarily in your left hand between your thumb and forefinger with the numbers on the harp facing you from left to right and ascending from 1 to 10. The harp should be held toward the back of the instrument so that your thumb and finger are as far away from the holes as possible. I call this "riding the ridge", the ridge being the back ridge of the cover plate. By holding it toward the back, you are assured that your finger and thumb will not interfere with your airflow into the harp and will allow for the harp to be placed deeper in your mouth.

The harp should be held in a relaxed yet firm manner. Your right and left hands should join together and form a cup around the harp. When you remove the harp from your lips it should look like you are catching water from a faucet. The thumb on your right hand can be used as a movable "latch" across the upper holes, or placed beside, underneath or behind the harp.

This cup impacts the tone. The tighter your seal, the more muted the sound and the more bass in your tone. As you release and open your right hand the tone becomes louder and brighter.

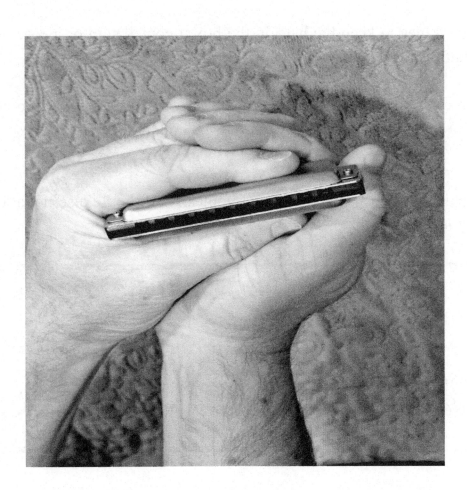

You Tube

It is time for our first You Tube demonstration. This one will focus on the proper way to hold the harp. The video is entitled "Tim Gartland on Harp Holding". You can search by title.

Care for the Harp

Never soak a harp in a liquid unless the manufacturer indicates it is ok to do so. It will temporarily make the harp easier to play, however after it dries it will be twice as hard to play and will reduce the harp's life.

It is a good idea to keep the harp in the box it comes with or a case designed to carry multiple harps.

You can clean the harp with a little water. If you are getting over a cold, it is a good idea to sterilize the harp by applying a liquid antiseptic to the holes on the comb.

You should not play anyone else's harmonica. You should also not allow anyone to play yours.

****SPOTLIGHT****

When you go to the music store, don't expect to be able to test drive different harps. It is against the law for retailers to sell a harp that has been used even once.

Highlights:

The harp is the only instrument you can make music by both blowing out and drawing in air.

Harps come in all twelve keys of music.

Harp players switch harps when songs are played in different keys.

The harp is held in your left hand between your left thumb and forefinger with the numbers on the harp facing you and ascending left to right from 1 to 10.

You can clean the harp with a little water.

Demonstration - (Track 2 on MP3's on my web site www.timgartland.com):

> ➤ Sound difference between harps in different keys

FAQs: How long does a harp last? Why do they need to be replaced?

Answer: With regular use and proper care, a harp can last six months to a year or more. What typically happens is that some of the notes begin sounding flat. Another symptom is that the reeds just start sounding dead. It becomes harder to play and the sound is less dynamic. I always check the tuning of my harps before a gig. You can check the tuning by checking the pitch of the notes with another musician's instrument or a guitar tuner.

Chapter 3

Searching for the Right Words:
Playing One Note at a Time

"The difference between the right word and the almost right word is the difference between lightning and a lightning bug."

– Mark Twain

When you first play the harp, you realize that you can play several notes at one time. But how do you play only one? The first step to becoming a harp player is being able to play a single note clearly and cleanly.

We will begin by learning the pursed lips method of playing a single note. Purse your lips as if you were preparing to make the sound "oooh". *When you make the "oooh" sound, the muscle that controls the narrowing of your mouth, the orbicularis oris, constricts to form a tight circle.* The inner edges of this circle are just inside your mouth. Your lips are further out, like the outer edge of a funnel. You do not play the harp with your lips. They are actually out of play and resting on the cover plate of the harmonica making contact with your finger and thumb. The orbicularis oris muscle is actually forming the inner most part of the circle in your mouth enabling you play one note.

Now take your harp and find the 4 hole, and study its size and the adjacent hole-separation slats. Place the forefingers of your hands over the 3 and 5 holes so that only the 4-hole and slats are exposed and gently blow out and draw in. Memorize the sound of harp notes played cleanly and clearly.

****SPOTLIGHT****

Here is a very important tip that you shouldn't forget. It takes a very small amount of air to vibrate the reeds of the harmonica correctly. Get in the habit early of gently blowing and drawing air.

Now without your forefingers blocking the holes and using the proper hand technique, raise the harp to your lips using the pursed lips method and practice smoothly playing the 4 blow (*blow as in blowing out air*) and 4 draw notes (*draw as in drawing in air).* Make sure you are placing the harp deep enough in your mouth. Your lips should be just touching your left index finger and thumb. Try and make a tight seal with your lips so no air escapes. Feel your orbicularis oris muscle pushing back (in an isometric way) against your hands ensuring that you have tight seal around the harmonica. If you hear air escape, then something is wrong. Either you are blowing or drawing too hard or your seal is not tight enough. You should never hear air escaping. You are creating an air chamber. The only opening in your mouth is over the hole you are playing.

Another point; make sure that you are not breathing through your nose when playing the harmonica.

****SPOTLIGHT****

Check your lip position on the harp by looking at yourself in the mirror. This will give you visual reinforcement that you are doing it right. Your mouth should look a little like the mouth of a fish. The mirror is useful when learning new techniques on the harp. I use one when I give lessons so that my students can benefit from seeing what they are learning.

Now experiment by playing the other nine holes as cleanly as the 4. Start by blowing holes 1 to 10 and then draw 1 to 10. Feel how each note requires a slightly different amount of air to play it cleanly. Part of the challenge of playing harp is making small adjustments for every note you play. The lower the number, the more air it takes.

The lower numbered holes, particularly the 2 draw, are difficult for most students to play clearly and cleanly. Drop your jaw and push it out to create a larger air chamber. This larger chamber allows you to blow and draw the additional air required to vibrate the longer reed.

As you begin to navigate up and down the harp, avoid removing the harp from your lips (except when you need to breath). Like the train and a train track, keep your mouth (the train) on the track (the harp). Glide the harp across your lips by moving your head not your hands. Maintain your pursed lips position as you glide to the next hole. Do not let the position collapse. Finally, keeping your lips moist will help you navigate smoothly.

Embouchure is the use of facial muscles and the shaping of the lips around a mouthpiece of a wind instrument. You are playing with an embouchure when you use the pursed lips method. Feel what your face muscles are doing. Use the pursed lips embouchure every time you practice so that you will start developing muscle memory in your lips and the muscles of your face.

Finally, think of the vowel sound "e" when you are playing single notes. When you make the "e", your tongue is naturally at the bottom of your mouth allowing the air to flow smoothly.

When I write music for the harp I use the plus sign (+) after the hole number to indicate notes that are blown. If the number has no (+) sign, then the hole is to be drawn. Here is the major scale in harp notation. This is the do-re-mi song. Play this until you can do it in your sleep. Notice the blow then draw pattern in holes 4 through 6 is reversed on the 7-hole. This is a fundamental change in the harp layout that continues through holes 8, 9 and 10.

Major Scale

Blow	Draw	Blow	Draw	Blow	Draw	Draw	Blow
4+	4	5+	5	6+	6	7	7+

Play it both going up to the 7 blow and back down to the 4 blow. Memorize this scale so that you do not have to read it.

Let's learn our first song, my interpretation of Eric Clapton's *Wonderful Tonight*.

Wonderful Tonight
Instrumental Section
4+ 5+ 4 4+ 4   4+ 5+ 4 4+ 2
4+ 5+ 4 4+ 4   5+ 5 6   6+

Verse
4+ 5+ 5 5+ 4 6+   4+ 5+ 5 5+ 5+ 4 4
4+ 5+ 5 5+ 4 6+   4+ 5+ 5 5+ 5+ 4 4
6 6 6 6+ 5+   5+ 5+ 5+ 6+ 4+
4 5+ 5   5 5+ 4 4 4+   3 4+

Bridge
5 6+ 6 6 6 6 4   4+ 5+ 5+ 5+ 6+ 4+
5 6+ 6 6 6 6 4   4 5+ 5 5+ 4 4+ 5+ 4   5+ 5+ 4 4+ 4+

Instrumental Section
4+ 5+ 4 4+ 4   4+ 5+ 4 4+ 2
4+ 5+ 4 4+ 4 5+ 5 6   6+

At this point, it is more important that you are playing one note well before moving on to mastering songs. However, if the above song does not inspire, go to www.harptabs.com. They have thousands of songs on the site.

There is no universal way to write music for harmonica. Some use the minus sign for draw notes for example. It is best to be flexible and play music for harp written in various ways.

You Tube

It is time for our second YouTube demonstration. This one will focus on the proper way to play one note. The video is entitled "Tim Gartland on Playing One Note on the Harp." You can search by title.

Here are a couple of final tips:

Remember to keep your lips moist. The moisture on your lips will help you slide the harp from hole to hole.

Keep your mouth dry. Too much moisture in your mouth will cause blockage in the holes of your harp and interfere with your breathing. Keep your mouth free of excess moisture by swallowing. Think about when you are in the dentist chair and that little device that helps keep the saliva to a minimum.

Make sure you are inhaling and exhaling exclusively through your mouth. While breathing through your nose is the preferred breathing method for most activities, harp playing is not one of them.

Highlights:

Play one note by pursing your lips like when you make the "oooh" sound.

It is important to keep this same-pursed lips position (embouchure) for all ten holes.

You do not play the harp with your lips.

The orbicularis oris muscle forms the inner most part of the circle in your mouth, which enables you play one note.

Get in the habit of gently blowing and drawing air.

You should never hear air escaping.

Keep your pursed lips position engaged as you glide from hole to hole.

Keep your tongue down in your mouth by thinking of the "e" sound.

Every note requires a slightly different amount of air to play cleanly.

You will develop muscle memory for this embouchure. It will be used whenever you pick up the harp going forward.

Memorize the major scale and play it both up and down.

Demonstrations (Track 3 on MP3's. All MP3's are on my website, www.timgartland.com):

> ➤ Playing the major scale and *Wonderful Tonight*

18

Chapter 4

Saying What You Are Feeling: Staccato and Legato Notes

"Music is your own experience, your own thoughts, your wisdom."

- Charlie Parker

Playing the harp or any instrument is ultimately about expressing yourself through your instrument. Now that you can play single notes cleanly, it is time to begin learning how to phrase your notes to say musically what you are feeling.

There are only 12 distinct notes in music; the beauty of music lies in all the different ways you can play them. So the sound of your notes and how you phrase them are as important as the notes you play. Two ways to phrase notes are to use either *staccato* or *legato*. *Staccato notes are short and distinct. Legato notes are long and connected.*

Playing Staccato

Say the soft "t" sound as in "cut". When you say cut, your tongue naturally rises to the top of your mouth and then back to its normal position. When the tongue rises, it helps to cut off the flow of air to the note you are playing. Once the tongue has reached the top, simultaneously cut off the air to the note. What you end up with is a very crisp, measured, succinct sound. Think of someone who speaks in a precise and clear manner and you will get the idea.

Cut is a great word to think of when learning to play staccato. In addition to its soft "t", the word itself reinforces the fact that when you play staccato you cut the note short.

Navigate up and down the harp playing staccato notes thinking of how you say the word cut.

I use this technique a lot in my playing. It is an excellent way to play fast runs because you can quickly end the note you playing and move to the next.

****Muscle Memory Drill****

Cut Drill: A great way to reinforce playing staccato is to say "cut" 10 times in sets of 3. This is also great general warm up for your mouth and tongue.

Now, let's get back to the major scale, this time playing it staccato. I know you have this memorized, but I wrote it down anyway.

Major Scale

Cut Blow	Cut Draw	Cut Blow	Cut Draw	Cut Blow	Cut Draw	Cut Draw	Cut Blow
4+	4	5+	5	6+	6	7	7+

Playing Legato

The word "hey" works best when learning to play legato notes on your harp.

When you say the word "hey" your tongue stays down in its natural position throughout the whole word.

When the tongue is down in its natural position, your notes on the harp are smooth and connected.

Try to keep the airflow steady as you alternate through the 4 blow and the 4 draw thinking of the word "hey."

Travel up and down the harp thinking of how you say the word hey and playing smooth connected legato notes.

Now play the first few notes of "Somewhere Over the Rainbow" using legato notes. At first you may find it challenging to jump from the 4 blow and land accurately on the 7 blow. Since we are playing legato and applying a steady stream of air, it is ok to blow a little of the 5 and 6 holes.

Somewhere Over the Rainbow

Hey Blow	Hey Blow	Hey Draw	Hey Blow	Hey Draw	Hey Draw	Hey Blow
4+	7+	7	6+	6	7	7+

21

Now let's play "Somewhere Over the Rainbow" in its entirety. The middle section should be played staccato and the beginning and end sections will be played legato.

Somewhere Over The Rainbow

Legato
4+   7+   7 6+ 6 7 7+ 4+ 6 6+

Legato
4+ 5 5+ 4+ 4 5+ 5 4 3 4+ 4 5+ 4+

Staccato
6+ 5+ 6+ 5+ 6+ 5+ 6+ 5+ 6+

Staccato   Legato
5 6+ 5 6+ 5 6+ 5 6+   6

Staccato
6+ 5+ 6+ 5+ 6+ 5+ 6+ 5+ 6+

Staccato   Legato
5 6+ 5 6+ 5 6+ 5 6+   6   7   8

Legato   Staccato
4+   7+   7   6+ 6 7 7+ 4+ 6 6+

Legato
4+ 5 5+ 4+ 4 5+ 5 4 3 4+ 4 5+ 4+

22

*****What hole are you playing?* ****

Carefully identify your starting hole number and place your mouth over it. As you begin playing a song and moving to different holes, track the hole number you are on. Always know what number hole you are playing throughout the song.

Highlights:

Staccato: Think of the soft "t" sound as in "cut".

Legato: Think of the word "hey" when learning to play legato notes on your harp.

Demonstration (Track 4 on MP3's):

➢ Demonstrate staccato and legato with the major scale and *Somewhere Over the Rainbow".*

All the MP3's are available on my website at www.timgartland.com.

Chapter 5

Talking with Your Hands: Hand Effects

"When you go to court you are putting your fate into the hands of twelve people who weren't smart enough to get out of jury duty."

- Norm Crosby

The Overall Importance of Your Hands

As mentioned, in general, you move your head versus your hands when navigating the harp. However, your hands are crucial in facilitating the music you play.

I cannot play the harp well if I have a halfhearted grip. If I am soloing on stage and have a certain musical passage in my head, I cannot play that passage without having a commanding grip.

Further, subtle adjustments of the angle of the harp to your embouchure can enhance your ability to play certain passages, techniques or even holes. Your wrist and hands are best at facilitating these adjustments.

In this chapter we are going to explore two major hand techniques used to create special effects. These techniques are easy to do and are instantly recognizable. They are the *wah-wah* and *fanning the harp*.

The Wah-Wah

Opening and closing the cup of your harp with your right hand while keeping the heels of your hands together to perform this technique. The speed is controlled by your right hand. Try this on the melody below.

4+ 4 5+ 6+ 5+ 4 4+

Fanning the Harp

Fanning is visually interesting, which is one of the only times we can say that when talking about harp playing. Take your right hand and pull it away from the harp and then return it rapidly and repeatedly. Try this on the same melody:

4+ 4 5+ 6+ 5+ 4 4+

Continue to experiment with these techniques. They definitely add a lot of color to your sound and can be used in countless musical passages.

The wah-wah and fanning the harp are the two main hand techniques. But there many others that create unique affects to color your music. Study the hands of masters like Sonny Terry and Sonny Boy Williamson II and you will pick up some other tricks of the trade.

Also, experiment with your own techniques. Do what works for you and you will create your own sound and celebrate the wonderful intrinsic qualities of the harmonica.

Highlights:

Open and close your right hand while keeping the heels of your hands together to perform the wah-wah.

Fanning the harp is when you take your right hand and pull it away from the harp and then return it rapidly and repeatedly.

You Tube

It is time for our third YouTube demonstration. This one will focus on hand effects. The video is entitled "Tim Gartland on Hand Effects". You can search by title.

Demonstration (Track 5 on MP3's):

➢ Demonstrate the wah-wah and fanning on the melody

Please subscribe to my YouTube Channel. There you will find all my educational and performance videos. You will also be notified every time I release a new video.

Chapter 6

Can I Say Something?: Playing Classic, Simple Songs

"Don't let it end like this. Tell them I said something."

- Poncho Villa from his death bed

The songs I have selected for you can be played using what we've learned so far. The first is the "Boogie-Woogie" melody. This is the not so secret formula for around 57,000 blues, R&B and rock and roll songs! This song is best played staccato style. Make sure you use the proper hand position and the pursed lips embouchure. Each note is the same length and equal to one beat. Try tapping your foot while playing this tune. One note, one beat, one-foot tap!

Boogie-Woogie (think of the word cut)

2 3 4 5+   2 3 4 5+   2 3 4 5+   2 3 4 5+

1+ 2+ 2 2+   1+ 2+ 2 2+

2 3 4 5+   2 3 4 5+

1 2+ 1 2+

1+ 2+ 2 2+

2 3 4 5+

2 3 4 5+

Here is my interpretation of "Blowing in the Wind".
Blowing in the Wind

6+   6+ 6+ 6   6 6   6+ 5+ 4 4+   5+ 6+   6+ 6+   6   6 6   6+

6+   6+ 6+ 6   6 6   6+ 5+ 4 4+   5+ 5 5 5+   4 4+ 4

6+   6+ 6+ 6   6 6   6+ 5+ 4 4+   5+ 6+ 6+ 6+   6 6 6   6+

5+ 5 5 5+ 4   4 5+ 5+ 5+ 4 4+

5+ 5 5 5+   4 4 4+ 3 4+

30

One of our main focuses thus far has been learning to play one note. Now let's introduce playing multiple notes in a musical way. You should find this a bit easier than the challenge of playing one note.

The harmonica was designed to play chords as well as single notes. *Chords are a combination of three or more notes that blend harmoniously when sounded together.* To play chords, open your mouth wide enough to play the 3 and 4 hole chords below. Note you have to open up more of the left side of your mouth to pick up the 1+ note on the 1+2+3+4+ blow chord below.

Rhythm to Blues

Draw Chord	Draw Chord	Draw Chord	Draw Chord	(eighth notes)
2-3-4	2-3-4	2-3-4	2-3-4	

Blow Chord   (quarter notes)
   1+2+3+4+

Draw Chord
   2-3-4

Blow Chord
   1+2+3+4+

Draw Chord
   2-3-4

Blow Chord
   1+2+3+4+

Draw Chord
   2-3-4

   Repeat

Most harp players play by ear instead of reading music. This is similar to the way we talk. You don't need to read from a script to have a great conversation with someone. It's the same with playing the harp. The key is to develop your harp vocabulary, songs and riffs you can play without reading them. With that in mind, practice these songs over and over so you can play them without looking at the notation. In other words, memorize them! Of course, while doing this, practice what we've learned so far. Hold the harp properly, use the lip purse embouchure, and play the notes cleanly, using legato and staccato.

I am sure you recognize the melody of at least one of these songs as well as the song's timing or tempo. The timing of the notes you play is just as important as hitting the right notes. The tempo of the song should maintain the same speed throughout the song. To help you maintain the tempo, tap your foot to the beat of the song as you play. The "Boogie Woogie" is a particularly good place to start tapping your foot. This version, as written, calls for you to tap your foot once for each note you play. Playing in rhythm does not get anymore straight forward than this.

****SPOTLIGHT****

I remember the first day I got a harp. It came with the notation to play the folk song "Oh Susanna". I played that song so many times I heard the song in my head as I fell asleep. I never had to read the notation for that song ever again.

As a bonus, here is the first song I learned way back when. The year was 1974 and I bought my first harmonica from money I earned as a paperboy for the Warren Tribune Chronicle in Warren, Ohio (this song is not on the MP3's).

Oh Susanna

4+   4   5+   6+   6+ 6 6+ 5+   4+

4   5+ 5+   4 4+   4

4+   4 5+   6+ 6+ 6   6+ 5+   4+

4   5+   5+   4   4   4+

5   5   6   6   6   6+   6+   5+   4+ 4

4+ 4 5+   6+   6+   6 6+ 5+ 4+ 4+

4   5+ 5+   4   4   4+

Highlights:

You are going to need to utilize your memory to play the harp.

Eventually you will be able to memorize countless songs without reading notation.

Tap your feet to maintain the tempo of the song

Demonstration (Track 6 on MP3's):

> ➤ Perform the songs *"Boogie Woogie", "Blowing In the Wind", and "Rhythm to Blues"*.

FAQ: Is there one best way to play a song, using either legato or staccato?

Answer: No. Although some songs lend themselves to either legato or staccato, experiment with both. Play it the way it sounds best to you. Your goal is interpret the song your own way.

Chapter 7

How Does This Sound?: The Tone of Your Playing

"A loud voice cannot compete with a clear voice, even if it's a whisper."

- Barry Neil Kaufman

The quality of the sound you get from your harp is what we call your tone. How important is tone? Think of a three-legged stool. It needs all three legs to work or you will land on your backside. Here are the three legs of harp playing:

1. The notes you play
2. The timing of the notes or phrasing
3. The tone of the notes

You need all three to be a complete harp player. These principles also apply to singing, and every musical instrument.

Let's start with your embouchure. Remember embouchure is the use of facial muscles and the shaping of the lips to the mouthpiece of a wind instrument. Proper embouchure allows the player to play all the notes of his instrument with a full and clear tone without fatiguing the muscles.

You need to work with your lips and facial muscles so that the muscles that form the pursed lips method are developed to the point that you have full control of them. Muscle memory comes into play here. With practice, your muscles will respond without thinking every time you pick up a harp.

****SPOTLIGHT****

I want you to take a second and think about the inside of your mouth. In the pursed lips position, feel the inside of your mouth and tongue. Feel the air as it passes through, feel the sensation. It helps you get connected to a part of your anatomy integral to harp playing.

Now, let's talk about *breathing*.

Start with your posture. If you slouch you are diminishing the capacity of your lungs. So sit up or stand straight when you are playing. Keep you rib cage lifted and supported at all times. Make sure when you are playing music from this book or any other source that it is on a music stand or otherwise in an elevated position. This will force you to stand up straight with your rib cage lifted.

Also, to open up the bottom of your lungs, make sure your hips are thrust slightly forward. When standing, have your knees bent slightly, like an athlete staying loose for the next play. Your stomach muscles should be taut.

Think of your lungs as two vessels that hold and pour water. When your lungs are full of air they are like the vessels topped off with water. When you talk, sing, or blow into the harp you are using your air like the vessel when you pour water from it. When you breathe in or draw in on the harp you are filling your lungs up like the vessel being filled with water. Because of nature of the hole layout on the harp, we tend to play more draw notes than blow notes, particularly as we learn to play blues, rock and country. Because of this, it is best to leave room in our lungs for this influx of air. To adjust to this fact, try to rebalance your lungs while playing so that your lungs are half full of air at all times.

How much air do you need to sing, talk or play harp? You need very little compared to the enormous capacity of your lungs. That's because your vocal chords, like the reeds of your harp, need only small controlled amounts of air to do their jobs at peak efficiency. Too much air and they lock up.

You may not believe this, but you can actually control the tone of your voice and your harp by directing the air from your lungs once it gets to your mouth cavity. The further back you direct your airflow in your head, the deeper and fuller your sound will be. If you direct your airflow towards your face, your sound becomes thinner or nasally. When you talk, sound is not created until the air you have summoned from your lungs hits your skull. You don't believe me? Talk while your hand is on your head and you can feel the vibrations. When playing the harp, try to make the notes resonate in the back of your skull. When you draw in, send the air back and up at a 45 degree angle. When you blow, bring the air from the back of your mouth.

The final and most crucial thing you need to do is to bring the air from the bottom of your lungs. You should sing and play from your *diaphragm*, which is the thick muscle separating your lungs from your gut. Keeping the lungs open through good posture sets this up. Flexing your diaphragm controls deep breathing or diaphragmatic breathing. This is also known as belly breathing because your belly expands when you inhale and deflates when you exhale (even when you are keeping the stomach muscles taut). Your chest should remain as fixed as possible supporting the lungs. This is the natural way to breath. The stress of everyday living turns us into chest breathers. Become a belly breather and you will be a happier, healthier person and have a great harp and vocal tone.

By playing from your diaphragm, you will have a reserve of power and a fuller tone. Shallower playing, using the air at the top of your lungs, yields less power, fewer musical options and a weaker tone.

****SPOTLIGHT****

Have you heard of the saying "belting out a song"? This refers to bringing air from your diaphragm. The singer is bringing the air from the lowest point in his or her lungs, which is near your belt line. Belting is associated with power and a deep rich singing voice. The same concept applies to playing the harp.

Listen to the MP3 and hear me play with a weak tone and then a full tone to The Beatles *Love Me Do.*

Love Me Do

```
5   5 +    4   2   2
5   5   5    5+  5  5+  4  2  2
```

You Tube

It is time for our next You Tube demonstration. This one will focus on breathing. The video is entitled "Tim Gartland on Breathing and Harp Playing". You can search by title.

Highlights:

Keep your lungs as open as possible, keep your chest lifted and stable, have good posture, push your hips slightly forward, bend your knees and keep your stomach muscles taut.

You need a small amount of air to play the harp compared to the enormous capacity for air in your lungs.

Bring the air from the bottom of your lungs, from your *diaphragm*.

Become a belly breather. Your belly should move when you breathe, not your chest.

Direct the column of air to the back of your skull for a deeper, warmer tone.

Demonstration (Track 7 on MP3's) :

➢ The song *"Love Me Do"* played with full tone versus weak tone

Chapter 8

Playing the Blues:
The 12 Bar Blues Form

"Blues is easy to play, but hard to feel."

–Jimi Hendrix

The blues form is a musical template or form that is instantly recognizable and is the foundation for rock and roll, country and rhythm and blues. In this chapter, you will be introduced to the twelve bar blues form and a blues scale that we can play with what we have learned so far.

The Blues Form

The standard blues form is made up of twelve measures or bars. What is a bar? *A bar is a segment of time with a fixed number of beats.* Most commonly, there are 4 beats per bar. This is best exemplified when a band member calls out at the beginning of the song "one, two, three, four." In this case, the member has counted out one bar, the four beats being marked by the count. The speed in which the member counts out the song determines the speed or tempo of the song that is about to be performed. Tapping your feet, snapping your fingers, clapping, etc. keep each of the four beats - one time for each beat. This is also known as *keeping time.*

The twelve bar blues utilizes three chords. These chords are referred to as the *one, four, five progression written as I, IV, V.* The I refers to the chord of the "key" the song is in.

Key is defined as the I chord, the I chord being the home chord which gives the song a sense of arrival, rest and release. The IV and V are four and five whole steps in music above the I. The IV and V chords provide tension and drama until the song comes back to or "resolves" back to the I chord.

The same letter values assigned chords identify song keys. In most songs, the first chord of the song is also the key the song is in, AKA, the "I".

There are seven main letters to identify song chords and keys. They start at A, like the alphabet and end at G. G is the z of the musical alphabet. They are:

A B C D E F G

If we were playing the blues in the key of C, then the I would be the C. IV and V chords would be F and G (you count the key you are in):

A B **C** D E **F** **G**
          I   IV V

If we were playing the blues in the key of A, then the I, IV and V chords would be A, D and E:

A B C **D** **E** F G
I   IV V

The most common chord and bar pattern for the twelve bar blues form is:

Four bars on the I chord
Two bars on the IV chord
Two bars back on the I chord
One bar on the V chord
One bar on the IV chord
One bar back on the I chord
One more bar back on the V chord

The bar counts above equals twelve. After you have finished these twelve bars, you would go to the start or "top" and that would start another "verse".

Here's an example of the twelve bar blues form in the key of C. On the top line is the chord letter value and I, IV, V designation.

C (I)	C (I)	C (I)	C (I)
Bar 1	Bar 2	Bar 3	Bar 4

F (IV)	F (IV)	C (I)	C (I)
Bar 5	Bar 6	Bar 7	Bar 8

G (V)	F (IV)	C (I)	G (V)
Bar 9	Bar 10	Bar 11	Bar 12

Now that we have a basic understanding of the blues form, how do we play the blues on the harmonica? Let's explain the pop and folk position first.

****Which key harmonica do I play? ****

When playing pop, folk, campfire type songs, the key the harmonica is in is the same as the key the song is in. This is called first position harmonica. It is also known as straight harp, as it is pretty straightforward. Say you want to play a song with a guitar player that is playing some pop or folk songs. Ask that person what key the song is in and grab a harp in that same key. Although you may only have a C harp now, harps come in all music keys.

Okay, first position is best suited for folk and pop, but what about the blues? The most popular way to play blues, country, rock and roll, and rhythm and blues on the harp is referred to as the second position or cross harp. *Second position is playing the harp four keys above the key the song is in.*

If the song were in C, you would use a harp in the key of F:

		1	2	3	**4**		
Keys:	A	B	C	D	E	**F**	G

If the song were in A, you would play a D harp and so on…

		1	2	3	**4**		
Keys:	A	B	C	**D**	E	F	G

Blues Scales

Scales are a series of ascending and descending notes that form the melodic foundation of music. There are many different types of scales in music. We learned the major scale earlier.

The blues scale is a marriage of African and Western musical cultures. It combines elements of the major scale with the so-called blue notes of the African American slaves and their descendants. This newly created scale is called the blues scale. *A blues scale contains the notes of the major scale except that the third, fifth and seventh notes of the major scale are lowered or flattened one half step on the piano.* The sonic effect is that the blues scale sounds more melancholy or sad. The notes that were lowered a half step are known as blues notes. They are also known as the minor or flattened third, fifth, and seventh notes because they are the third, fifth and seventh notes of the major scale lowered one half step (one piano key; example moving from a white key down to a black).

Here is a simplified blues scale using the techniques we have learned so far. It is simplified because at this point we are only playing one blue note, the minor seventh note (5 draw). In the next two chapters we will learn an exciting technique called bending which will enable you to play new notes on the harmonica. These bend notes include notes on the 3 and 4 hole draw notes which will enable us to play the minor third and fifth blue notes and complete the blues scale as described above.

It is time to pick up, if you do not have already, a harmonica in the key of A. The "A" harmonica is the most popular harmonica to play the blues on.

Here is the Simple Blues Scale with an A keyed harp:

(+ = Blow)

E	G#	A	B	D	E
2	3	4+	4	5	6+

Let's use this scale over a blues song written on the next page. Note that the chord and bar numbers are written over the harmonica hole numbers. Also note that the song's first chord is an E chord, which is the key the song is in. Remember, we are now using an A harp. Since we are playing the blues, we are going to play in the second position. The song key and harp selection are confirmed below:

The song on the next page is in the key of E, so we will use an A harp.

				4			1	2	3
Keys:				**A**	B	C	D	E	F	G

Simple Scale Strut

|E Chord (Bar 1)| |E Chord (Bar 2)|
  6+   +6   6+ 6+ 5+ 4 3 2

|E Chord (Bar 3)| |E Chord (Bar 4)|
  6+   6+   6+ 6+ 5+ 4 3 2

|A Chord (Bar 5)| |A Chord (Bar 6)|
3 4+ 3 4+ 4 3   3 4+ 3 4+   4

|E Chord (Bar 7)| |E Chord (Bar 8)|
  6+ 6+ 5+ 4   3   2 2

|B Chord (Bar 9)| |A Chord (Bar 10)|
4   4 4   4+   4+ 4+

|E Chord (Bar 11)| |B chord (Bar 12)|
2   2+ 2 2+   2   1

Here's a final, related tip to remember where you are in the song. To know where you are, you can count bars. The tip is to add one number to the first beat of every bar you count.

                  Bar 1:   **1** 2 3 4
                  Bar 2:   **2** 2 3 4
                  Bar 3:   **3** 2 3 4
                  Bar 4:   **4** 2 3 4   (your on the fourth bar)

And so on…

You Tube

It is time for our next YouTube demonstration. This one will focus on the 12 Bar Blues. The video is entitled "Tim Gartland with the 12 Bar Blues". You can search by title.

Highlights:

I, IV, V refers to the relationship between the key the song is in and the fourth and fifth whole step above it.

In 4/4 time, there are 1,2,3,4 quarter note beats per bar.

First position is playing the harp in the same key the song is in

Second position is playing the harp four keys above the key the song is in.

Demonstration (Track 8 on MP3's):

- ➤ Simple blues scale
- ➤ The song "Simple Scale Strut"

FAQ: Are all blues songs played the same way?

Answer: No. There are many, many different ways to play them. Some are slow, fast, have different rhythms, major or minor chords etc. But they all have to be played with feeling!

Chapter 9

Reeding is Fundamental: Introduction to Bending Notes

"We all do 'do, re, mi,' but you have got to find the other notes yourself."

-Louis Armstrong

A fundamental technique for playing the harp is learning how to bend reeds to hit notes not available when playing the harp normally.

This is one of the most challenging and rewarding parts of learning the harp. This technique is commonly referred to as *bending notes*. I prefer calling it bending reeds. *By adding air pressure to bend the reed you reach notes on the harmonica that are available between the normal blow and draw notes in each hole.* Once again the piano analogy is useful: without bending you can play only the white keys, a diatonic scale; with bending you can play all the notes in between, a chromatic scale.

Diatonic Scale (white piano keys): C-D-E-F-G-A-B
Chromatic Scale (both white and black keys): C-C#-D-D#-E-F-F#-G-G#-A-A#-B

Sharp and Flat Notes

Some notes in the scale can be referred by two names. For example, the note C sharp is the exact same note as the D flat (the "#" symbol is used to indicate sharp notes and the "b" is used to indicate flat notes). All the black keys on the piano can be referred to by two names. Relative to the C note, C# is a half note higher, so from the C note's "perspective", it is a C#. From the D note's "perspective" that same note is a half note lower, so the D note refers to it as the Db. See amplified example below:

From the C note	**up one piano key (half step)**	**to the D note (whole step)**
Note name: C	C# is also know as Db	D

In this chapter we will introduce note bending on the first six holes of the harmonica. We will talk about bending on holes 7 through 10 later on in the guide.

We bend the first 6 holes by drawing in air versus holes 7 through 10, which are bent by blowing out. Playing the harp without bending provides only seven notes (the diatonic scale). Through bending, we will now be able to play all twelve notes in the chromatic scale. Here is an illustration of the notes that are possible on the A harp.

	1	2	3	4	5	6	7	8	9	10
Full Note Bend										G
Half Note Bend								C	D#	G#
Blow	A	C#	E	A	C#	E	A	C#	E	A
A HARP	1	2	3	4	5	6	7	8	9	10
Draw	B	E	G#	B	D	F#	G#	B	D	F#
Half Note Bend	A#	D#	G	A#		F				
Full Note Bend		D	F#							
Full and 1/2 Bend			F							

Diatonic Scale in the Key of A: A-B-C#-D-E-F#G#

Chromatic Scale in the Key of A: A-A#-B-C-C#-D-D#E-F-F#-G-G#

Notice that the notes you can bend are found in between the normal blow and draw notes for each numbered hole. Example: 3 Blow is E and 3 Draw is G#. Through draw bends on the 3-hole, you can play the notes in between E up to G#, F, F# and G.

Let's look at the 4 draw. This is a B note. The 4 blow is the A note so there is a half step available in the middle, the A# note. Play the 4 draw while your mouth is in the position to make the vowel sound "e". To bend the 4 draw, think of saying the vowel sound 'oooh". (You are not actually saying the vowel sounds while you are playing, just approximating the mouth, lip and jaw positions.)

When your mouth is the same as the "oooh" position, curl the tip of your tongue back and up toward the roof of your mouth (but not touching the roof of your mouth). This constricts the airflow in your mouth. By taking in air at the same rate through a smaller space you increase the air pressure. This added pressure forces the reed to bend producing the A#.

51

Try to sing the B (4 draw) and A# (4 draw bend) notes using the corresponding vowel sounds. Audio examples of this are available on Track 9 on MP3's. It is helpful to hear the note you are trying to reach on the harp before you try it. This is similar in sports to visualizing what you are about to try before doing it.

Now, raise the harp to your mouth and think of the vowel sounds "e" then "oooh" while drawing in on the 4. *Do not give in to the tendency to draw in more air on the bend to force the note.* Trust the tongue and mouth positions to create the added pressure needed for the bend.

Once you reach the bend, hold it as long as you can. This will help your tongue, jaw and mouth muscles to create muscle memory. It will also help you to get the proper feel of your mouth position to achieve the bend. You will feel pressure, as the reed does not want to stay where you want it. Remember we are creating notes that were not originally contemplated to be played on this instrument.

Stay focused on the 4 draw bend. Be patient. Try not to take in too much air. If it is not working set it aside for a while and come back to it. You are going to get it; it's just a matter of time and effort before you perfect it.

Let's build on the 4 draw bend with an exercise that will help you reinforce the importance of what you just learned. The 4 draw bend in the second position (A Harp in the Key of E) is the *flatted or minor 5th*, or one of the all important "blue notes" contained in the blues scale. Minor notes evoke the deep emotions associated with the blues. Here we will use the ½ sign to indicate the half note bend. Try this riff below:

4 Draw Bend Exercise:

2   3   4 4½ 4 4½ 4 3 2

Now let's use the 4½ draw in a song:

Half Bend Blues

E Chord Bar 1   E Bar 2
4 4½ 4 4½ 3 2   4 4½ 4 4½ 3

E Bar 3   E Bar 4
4½ 4 4½ 4 4+   3   2

A Bar 5   A Bar 6
4+ 4+ 3 4+ 4 2   4+ 4 + 3 4+ 4

E Bar 7   E Bar 8
4   4½ 4 4½   3 2 2

B Bar 9   A Bar 10
4 4½ 3 4   3 4 4+

E Bar 11   B Bar 12
2 2+ 2 2 2+ 2 2   1 1

**** *SPOTLIGHT* ****

When you first practice bending notes, you will create some interesting sounds that might call into question the wisdom of this musical endeavor even to those whose love is unconditional. If you can't find a quiet place where you can practice in private, use the hand techniques in Chapter 1 to surround the harp and mute the sound. Also practice bending using the least amount of air possible to reduce the volume and practice your breath control.

Highlights:

By taking air at the same rate through a smaller space you increase the air pressure. This pressure forces the reed to bend.

Think of the vowel sound "oooh" while drawing in on the 4 hole for the half note bend.

Trust the vowel sounds and the position your mouth is forming to create the added pressure.

The tongue is moving up and back when bending the 4 draw.

Don't get frustrated. This is the hardest technique to master on the harp.

Demonstration (Track 9 on MP3's):

> ➤ 4 draw and 4 draw bend
> ➤ 4 Draw Bend Exercise
> ➤ The song "Half Bend Blues"

FAQ: Who invented the twelve bar form?

Answer: It actually was used in folk songs in Europe hundreds of years ago. It was imported to America, and African-Americans created the blues by adding percussive rhythms and blue notes (minor tonalities) to the melodies.

Chapter 10

Deep Discussions:
Advanced Note Bending

"The little reed, bending to the force of the wind, soon stood
upright again when the storm passed over."

-Aesop

Now we are going to head into the deepest depths of harp playing techniques. In this chapter, we will learn how to reach the deeper draw bends in holes 1 through 6. We will introduce two additional vowel sounds to reach the deeper bends. Let's look again at the notes available through bending:

Full Note Bend										G
Half Note Bend								C	D#	G#
Blow	A	C#	E	A	C#	E	A	C#	E	A
A HARP	1	2	3	4	5	6	7	8	9	10
Draw	B	E	G#	B	D	F#	G#	B	D	F#
Half Note Bend	A#	D#	G	A#		F				
Full Note Bend		D	F#							
Full & ½ Bend			F							

The 6 draw bend, like the 4 draw bend is played by thinking of the vowels "e" for the normal 6 draw and then the "oooh" for the bend. The normal 6 draw with an A harp is F#, the draw bend is F. Like the 4 draw the tongue is curled up and back.

Practice on the 6 draw. Feel the pressure it takes to make the bend. The tongue is curled up and goes back, but not as far as it does with the 4 draw bend.

Really practice the 4 and 6 bends before moving on. Next, make sure you can hit the notes legato and staccato style. For staccato playing while bending notes, think of "tee" for the normal note and "toooh" for the bent note. For legato style, think of the h as in "he" for the normal note and "hooh" for the bent note.

Let's go down to the 1 draw. Like holes 4 and 6, the 1 draw has only a half note bend available.

The 1-hole has the lowest notes; therefore it has the longest reeds, so we need to apply more air pressure. This is accomplished by creating a bigger open space in your mouth. Drop your jaw and protrude it forward while maintain your embouchure. This increases the volume of air needed to properly vibrate the lower, longer reeds. As you move up the harp you will incrementally move your jaw up and back for the higher notes with the smaller reeds. Kind of like the difference between chugging water (wide open mouth space, lower reeds) and sipping tea (narrow mouth space, higher reeds).

For the 1 draw we will once again think of the "e" sound for the normal draw and we will introduce the "o" sound for the draw bend (not the "oooh"). The "o" creates the added pressure needed to cleanly hit the 1 draw bend. When you make the "o" sound, it forces your tongue down and back (versus curled up and back with the 4 and 6 bends) and your jaw is lower and more forward than when you make the "oooh."

Once again, take your time with this and all the other bends. Each hole presents a different challenge. Each bend requires a slightly different tongue and jaw position. The 1 draw bend can be more difficult than the 4 and the 6. Once you get it, practice it over and over and build muscle memory. Remember to listen to the MP3 track to hear how the notes sound.

There are two draw bends on the 2-hole. With the normal draw note you have the E, a half note below is the D# and the whole note bend is a D. The D is the same as the 5 draw, only an octave lower. The cool thing about the half note draw is that the D# is not available anywhere else in holes 1 through 6.

With the 2 hole, think of the "e" sound for the 2 draw, back to the "oooh" sound for the half note bend and the "o" sound for the full note bend.

Sing the notes using the "e," "oooh" and "o" sounds.

Let the vowel sounds and tongue and jaw positions do the work. If you are not getting it, focus harder on making sure your mouth is in the proper vowel sound position for each bend. Just like the 4 and 6 bends the half note bend requires the tongue to curl up and back. The 2 full bend like the 1 draw require the tongue and jaw to move down and back.

Once again use the soft "t" sound as in "cut" for the staccato treatment of these notes; "te," tooh and "toe". For legato, use the h sound as in "he," "hooh" and "hoe".

Now, let's move on to the third hole. Think of the "e" sound for the 3 normal draw, the "oooh" sound for the half step bend, the "o" sound for the full note bend, and finally we introduce the "ahh" sound for the note and half bend. Yes, it is the same as open and up a say "ahh" at the doctor's office. The "ahh" sound forces the tongue further back and the jaw even lower than the "o." These notes are G#, G, F# and F. Again, all the bend notes can be heard on the MP3.

Once again, sing the notes with the vowel sounds so you can hear the notes you are trying to reach. There is an old saying that if you don't know where you are going, any place will do. If you can't hear or, with the use of a tuner see the note you are trying to play, you won't know if you are hitting it or not. Use the MP3 to hear the notes. Have those notes in your head before you play them. Once you hit the bend hold it and feel where your mouth is positioned. That will help you to make the connection and develop muscle memory.

This is going to take some practice. Don't get frustrated. You will get this. It's all about the vowel sounds and the tongue and jaw positions. Don't try to blow harder as the reed will lock up.

Here is a helpful diagram that references the numbered holes with the notes and the vowel sounds needed to play the bends:

	Note	Vowel Sound	Note	Vowel Sound	Note	Vowel Sound	Note	Vowel Sound	Note	Note	Vowel Sound
Hole Number	1	1	2	2	3	3	4	4	5	6	6
Draw Notes	B	"E"	E	"E"	G#	"E"	B	"E"	D	F#	"E"
Half Note Bend	A#	"O"	D#	"Ooh"	G	"Ooh"	A#	"Ooh"		F	"Ooh"
Full Note Bend			D	"O"	F#	"O"					
Full and half					F	"Ahh"					

Remember, bending the reeds on harmonica to play additional notes is one of the most challenging aspects of playing the harmonica. It is not something that you can master and then stop working at it. Even today, after 30 plus years of playing, I work on playing these bends in tune and with fluidity in a musical context. The most scientific way I know to tell if your bends are in tune is to use a tuner.

**** *Tuner*****

Pick up a guitar tuner on line or at a music store. You can also download an app for your smart phone. It should have a display to indicate the note you are playing on the screen. It will also have a meter that tells you if you are flat or sharp or in perfect pitch with the note you are playing. While perfect pitch is the goal, declare victory when the screen shows you have played the note you are seeking to bend.

Here are some exercises for you to practice to.

Bending Exercises:

#1
4   4½   4   4½   4

#2
6   6½   6   6½   6

#3
1   1½   1

#4
2   2½   2full   2½   2

#5
3   3½   3full   3full½   3full   3½   3

#6
3½   3   4   4+   3½   2

#7
1   2full   2   3½   2

#8
1   2+   2   3½   3full   2

Now let's play a blues song using the bends we have learned.

Bent But Not Broke

E Chord Bar 1
2 3½ 3½ 2 2full 2 2

E Bar 2
3½ 3½ 2 2full 2

E Bar 3
3½   3½ 2 2full 2

E Bar 4
 1   2 2full

A Bar 5
4+ 4+ 3½   4+ 4 3 2

A Bar 6
4+ 4+ 3½ 4+ 4 1 2+

 E Bar 7 *
 3½ 3½ 2 2full 2 2

E Bar 8
 2

B Bar 9
4 4 4½ 3 4 4

A Bar 10**
4+ 4+ 3½ 3½ 2 2

E Bar 11
 2 3½ 3½ 2

B Bar 12
2full 2 1 2+ 2

*The 1 and the 2+ notes before Bar 7 are pick-up notes. *Pick-up notes are notes that precede the first beat in a bar. They add a rhythmic, percussive element to music.*

61

You Tube

It is time for our next YouTube demonstration. This one will focus on bending. The video is entitled "Tim Gartland on Bending Notes on the Harp". You can search by title.

Note: There are even more advanced bends called "overblows" which are not covered in this book. For more information on "overblows", check out the internet.

Highlights:

Before trying to bend, reference the pitches by singing or playing them.

For half note bends the tongue curls up and back; for full and full ½ bends, the tongue moves back and down.

The 6 draw like the 4 draw is played by emulating the vowels "e" then "oooh."

For the 1 draw we will once again think of the "e" sounds for the normal 1 draw and introduce the "o" sound for the draw bend (not the "oooh").

There are two draw bend notes on the 2-hole. Use "ooh" then "o."

There are three draw bends in the 3-hole. Use "oooh," "o," and a new vowel sound "ahh."

Demonstration (Track 10 on MP3's):
> ➢ Demonstrate bending exercises
> ➢ Demonstrate blues song "Bent but Not Broke"
> ➢ Demonstrate the 1,2,3 and 6 hole bends with vowel sounds

Chapter 11

Could You Use It In A Sentence?
10 Classic Harp Riffs

"Great melody over great riffs is, to me, is the secret of it all."

-Steven Tyler, Aerosmith

Words are to sentences in language what notes are to *riffs* in music. This chapter will introduce musical sentences or riffs. *Riffs are defined as melodic phrases.*

Riffs can be a central theme of a song or solo, the beginning and possible ending of the piece with improvisation in between. Riffs can also be linked together to form much of the body of the solo, touchstones between more free form musical sections. Soloing often involves the concept of making variations on a theme. The opening riff, the theme, is often repeated with subtle note or timing variations. Listen for this as you listen to soloists of all types, particularly in jazz, blues and rock and roll.

There are so many cool riffs that are part of the harp vocabulary it's almost impossible to solo without quoting someone's riff. Riffs are important to learn, memorize, and add to your vocabulary. Hopefully, they will lead you to create your own unique contribution to the musical conversation.

Here is my interpretation of some classic riffs on the harp that you should learn to play fluently. As always, use your ears and your brain to memorize these. Try memory devices to learn these riffs. Study hole numbers and bends for each.
Again the + equals blow notes. Notation for reed bends are: " ½" equals the half note bend, "full" equals a full note bend and "full½ " equals a note and a half bend.

		Vowel		Vowel		Vowel		Vowel			Vowel
	Note	Sound	Note	Sound	Note	Sound	Note	Sound			Sound
Hole Number	1	1	2	2	3	3	4	4	5	6	
Draw Notes	B	"E"	E	"E"	G#	"E"	B	"E"	D	F#	"E"
Half Note Bends	A#	"O"	D#	"Ooh"	G	"Ooh"	A#	"Ooh"		F	"Ooh"
Full Note Bends			D	"O"	F#	"O"					
Note and a Half					F	"Ahh"					

10 Famous Harp Riffs (remember to listen to the MP3 examples)

Riff 1

 3   3   3   3   3 4+ 4   2   3 4+ 3   2
2full (5 times)   2full (5 times)   2full   2
Riff from War's "Low Rider"

Riff 2

2full   2   4+   3½   2   2full   2 (repeat)
2full   2   3½   2
Riff from the Rolling Stones "Miss You"

Riff 3

4 4   4 5+ 4+ 5   5   5   5+   5   5+
4 4   4 5+ 4+ 5   5
Riff from The Romantics "What I Like About You"

Riff 4

1   2   3   4   4½   4
Riff from Jimmy Reeds "Ain't Got You"

Riff 5

2   4+   3½   2   1   2full   2full   2
Muddy Water: "Mannish Boy" combined with "Hoochie Coochie Man"

Riff 6

 2   2   2 3½   2   2 2full   1   2full 2full   1   1½
R.L. Burnside's F.M. radio hit "It's Bad You Know"

Riff 7

1 2+ 1   2   3½   3½ 3full 3full   2   2full   2
Riff from "Sweet Home Chicago"

Riff 8

2   2full 2 2full 1   11/2   1+   2   2full   2

Taj Mahal's "The Cuckoo"

Riff 9

2   3½   2   3½   2   2   2   3½   2 3½   2   2full

From the blues song "Baby Please Don't Go"

Riff 10

2   3½   3   4   5+   6+   6+

Opening riff from Little Walters instrumental "Juke"

Ok, so now you got ten classic riffs to work with. Memorize these. They will give you some ideas for your own riffs and help you master the techniques learned so far, which includes playing one note cleanly, staccato and legato, and bending notes.

Don't fret if you can't play these perfectly right away. Chip away at them as you have time. Revisit them again and again and keep trying to improve your performance. The journey is the thing with most challenges, and definitely with this one.

Highlights:

These riffs should be memorized.

Use your ears and your brain and file them away so that you can play them without looking at the notation.

Demonstration (Track 11 on MP3's):

> ➤ Perform all the riffs

FAQ: Where do harmonica players get their ideas for riffs?

Answer: Other harp players, as well as horn players, guitar players, other instruments etc.

Here is a picture of legendary harp player Lazy Lester and I, Austin, Texas, 2015.

Chapter 12

High Talker:
Playing the Upper Register of the Harp

"The rung of the ladder was never meant to rest upon, but only to hold a man's foot long enough to enable him to put the other somewhat higher."

-Thomas Henry Huxley

In this chapter we will focus on the upper register of the harp, holes 6 through 10. This is an underplayed part of the harp, which is a shame because it offers a third octave of music in which you can play.

Before hitting those high notes, the first thing you need to know is that the note sequence on the harp switches with hole 7. In holes 1 through 6 the blow note is lower than the draw note. In holes 7 through 10 the blow note is higher.

Blow Notes	A	C#	E	A	C#	E	A	C#	E	A
	1	2	3	4	5	6	7	8	9	10
Draw Notes	B	E	G#	B	D	F#	G#	B	D	F#

Let's start by playing the major scale in the upper register in the second position.

6+ 6 7 7+ 8 8+ 9 9+

Notice that the first and last notes of the scale (6+ and 9+) are E notes. We are playing an E major scale on the A harmonica. Four keys up from E is the A. We are playing an A harmonica, the scale is in E, so we are playing in the second position (Second position = Harp four keys above the key/scale of the song).

When you play the higher notes it takes a smaller more focused volume of air to vibrate the reeds. That's because the reeds are shorter.

Think of your mouth cavity as an air chamber. In the upper register it takes less air so decrease the volume of air in your mouth by raising your jaw and tongue. This should provide a narrow more focused airflow to vibrate the smaller reeds in the upper register. Once again, think of the "sipping hot tea analogy".

Now let's play the major scale in the second position in two octaves (remember to incrementally decrease your mouth cavity as you navigate up the harp by moving you jaw back and up and tongue up):

2 3full 3 4+ 4 5+ 5 6+ 6 7 7+ 8 8+ 9 9+

70

Here's a blues riff using the higher register:

6+   7   8   8+   9+   9+

This riff can be played in two octaves:

2   3   4   5+   6+   6 +   6+   7   8   8+   9+   9+

Here are more upper register blues riffs:

#1
9+   9   8   9+   9   8   9   9+

#2
8   9   9+   9   8   9   9+

#3
6 +   7   8   8+   9+   9+   9   8+   8   8+

#4
8   9   8   8+   9   8

Upper Register Bends

The 8, 9 and 10 blow note reeds can be bent. The 8 and 9 holes have half note bends and the 10 hole has both a half note and a whole note bend. The C harp is about the highest pitched harp on which you can bend the upper register notes. As you move to the higher pitched harps, the reeds are just too small to bend. The upper register bends get easier as you go down to harps in the keys of B, Bb, A, Ab, and finally the lowest tuned harp, the G harp.

Below is the note layout with the upper register bends for an A harp.

Full bend										G
Half bend									C	D#	G#
Blow Notes	A	C#	E	A	C#	E	A	C#	E	A
A HARP	1	2	3	4	5	6	7	8	9	10
Draw Notes	B	E	G#	B	D	F#	G#	B	D	F#

Start by playing the 8 note softly and cleanly. Now simply move your tongue forward and down from this position toward the harp while maintaining your embouchure. As the tongue moves forward, the tip ends up bumping against the back of the lower teeth. This movement of the tongue reduces the size of the air chamber in your mouth. *By blowing with constant pressure though a smaller space you create the needed extra pressure to bend the reed.*

Once the reed bends, hold your tongue in place and hold the note. You will feel pressure. Hold against the pressure. Check to see if you are hitting the pitch of the bend correctly with the tuner. Use muscle memory to remember where the tongue needs to be to bend the reed. Once you hit the note, alternate between the 8 normal and the 8 bend. Try hitting it staccato and legato style.

Just a word about bent notes in general. Remember they were not designed to be played on the diatonic harp. Once you can play them in pitch, they really want to release back to the normal note for the hole. Your job is to hold that note in the proper pitch and with control. It's like training a wild horse.

Next try the 9 hole, which is a similar bend to the 8. The tongue is humped, raised in the back more than with the 8 bend. The tip of the tongue is still behind the lower teeth. Again check pitch and keep working on it until you can control it.

Now let's move to the 10-hole half note bend. The tongue is once again slightly more humped in the back than the 9 and here we need to add a little more force, a little more air pressure to make this smallest of reeds bend. Don't overdo it by blowing too much air. Just use a controlled increase of force. Now try the 10 full bend, the tongue should be humped even more and even more force added. These bends can be quite challenging but offer a nice return for your efforts in your soloing.

Upper Register with Bends

#1
8+ 8½+ 8+ 8½+ 8+ 9+

#2
9+ 9½+ 9+ 8+ 7+

#3
10+ 10+full 10+

#4
9½+ 9+ 9½+ 9+ 9½+ 9+

#5
8½+ 8+ 9+ 9 8 9 9+

****SPOTLIGHT****
I often utilize the upper register towards the end of my solo. The higher notes add to a dramatic flourish if that's what is needed for the song.

Highlights:

In holes 1 through 6 the blow note is lower than the draw note. In holes 7 through 10 the blow note is higher.

In the upper register it takes less air so decrease the volume of air in your mouth by raising your jaw and tongue

To bend the higher notes, move your tongue forward and up towards the harp.

Use harps in keys G through C when bending the upper register notes.

 The A harp is by the most popular key to bend notes in the upper register

Demonstration (Track 12 on MP3's):

> ➢ Upper register blues riffs
> ➢ Upper register blues riffs with bends

FAQ: Why don't more harp players use the upper register (holes 6 to 10) more?

Answer: It could be because of the reversal of the note sequence beginning in hole 7. Also, it is harder to get a full, warm tone with the higher notes.
More and more players are playing in the upper register now. John Popper's (Blues Traveler) influence has helped encourage players to explore the high notes melodies and riffs.

Chapter 13

Speaking In Tongues: Tongue Blocking and Tongue Slapping

"Let your tongue speak what your heart thinks."

–Davy Crockett

Using your tongue to play the harp is an important part of becoming a good harp player. In this chapter we are going to use the tongue to learn the techniques of *tongue blocking* and *tongue slapping*.

Tongue Blocking

Tongue blocking is an additional way to play single notes. Tongue blocking provides you with a number of advantages. The advantages include adding chords to your single note playing through a technique called tongue slapping as well as the ability to play octaves. The former will be described later in this chapter and the latter will be covered in the next.

Now, let's learn to tongue block single notes. This is of course a different embouchure than the purse lip approach. It is much more relaxed. Start by opening your mouth just wide enough to cover the first four holes. Using the top of your tongue, place the area just before the tip on the harp. This area is found right as the tongue begins to narrow. The tongue slightly protrudes over the bottom teeth. It's kind of like you are in the early stages of sticking your tongue out at somebody.

Get the feel of how the tongue feels over the holes. Using your tongue, block holes 1 through 3 with your tongue and play 4+ blowing out of the right side of your mouth.

Take some time with this until you can do this smoothly. Don't be too hard on your tongue if it does not immediately do what you want it to do. Once again, you are asking a part of your body to do something that it has never done before. It will take some time to build muscle memory but you (and your tongue) will get there.

Now hold the tongue in place and play the 4 draw. Make sure you can hit the 4+ and 4 cleanly.

The degree of difficulty of learning this technique is similar to learning how to bend notes. They are the two most challenging harmonica techniques. It is not easy to do, but stick with it and you will get it. It is classic example of mind over matter. If your brain keeps telling your tongue what to do, it will eventually get used to this new gig.

Now, play the major scale from 4+ to 9+ tongue blocking all the way:

4+ 4 5+ 5 6+ 6 7 7+ 8 8+ 9 9+

Tongue Slapping

Tongue slapping is when you play a chord and then immediately slap the tongue on three of the holes and play a single note. Think of the rhythm when you say "ta-da" and you will get the idea of the rhythm (as always check the CD/MP3 as well). Briefly adding the chord before the note gives your playing a nice full effect, like the sound of an organ or accordion.

Again, open up your mouth wide enough to blow holes 1+ through 4+. This is a major chord. Now move your tongue forward and block holes 1 to 3 and blow out only on the 4+ hole from the right side of your mouth (just like when you tongue block). You want to hit the full chord then the single note cleanly. Practice so that you can do this in rapid succession.

Let's practice tongue slapping with the on the simple scale exercise below:

Blow Chord 1+- 4+   then   4+

Draw Chord 1- 4   then   4

Blow Chord 2+-5+   then   5+

Draw Chord 2-5   then   5

Blow Chord 3+- 6+   then   6+

Then go right back down the scale:

Chord 3+-6+   6+

Chord 2-5   5

Chord 2+-5+   5+

Chord 1-4   4

Chord 1+-4+   4+

Once again, set reasonable expectations for mastering these techniques. It is not easy. About this time I always remind my students how playing the harp is surprisingly sophisticated. This is something that could take a while to perfect but once again provides a big payoff. You will gain even more separation from the beginner/intermediate player.

Tongue Blocking Vs. Lip Pursing

We are going to utilize both tongue blocking and the pursed lips method as integral parts of our playing. Before we go into when we tongue block versus lip purse, let's discuss the alternatives of employing one or the other methods exclusively.

Can I just employ the pursed lips method?

There is a school of players who lip purse nearly 100 percent of the time. They bend notes, the whole bag of tricks, by lip pursing. From this school there are many great players who have made brilliant music on the harp with the pursed lips method.

A couple of limitations are that you can't tongue slap chords or play octaves (introduced in the next chapter).

Can I just employ the tongue blocking method?

Another school of players tongue blocks nearly 100 percent of the time. They tongue block all ten holes, bend notes and perform the entire repertoire of techniques with the tongue blocking technique. In fact many of the all time greats tongue blocked exclusively.

A couple of advantages to the pursed lips method are that it's easier to hit the note bends and the pursed lips tone can be very cool and useful in many places.

Why should I employ both methods?

Employing both techniques gives the player the best of both worlds. One of the true giants of blues harp, Big Walter Horton, is a leader of this style of playing. Modern harp master and educator Jerry Portnoy is also an advocate and teacher of this approach.

When do I lip purse and when do I tongue block?

I have a way of integrating the two techniques that has worked for me and will work for you as well. It involves alternating between the two, following a couple of general rules.

General Rule #1 for Alternating

1 to 3 holes = pursed lips   4 to 10 = tongue blocking

Tongue blocking and slapping holes 4 through 10 improves the tone of notes as you travel up to these higher holes because they are naturally thinner sounding than holes 1 through 3. Blocking allows you to supplement these notes with chords and octaves.

General Rule #2 for Alternating

Note bends = pursed lips

I find bending notes with the pursed lips method to be easier and that it provides more flexibility to perform faster runs on the harp.

One exception to the General Rule #1 is that you also lip purse the bends in holes 4 through 10. Also, if I am making a quick run up to the 4 to 10 holes I may stick with the pursed embouchure. Hey, making music on the harp sometimes involves bending rules as well as reeds.

Okay, now we are going to be playing with both embouchures. So how do we switch between the two? When we switch back and forth between tongue blocking to lip pursing, the mouth goes from a four-hole open and relaxed position to a more closed, pursed/flexed single hole one. Switching back and forth with fluidity will take some time. How do you accomplish this? The same way you get to play Carnegie Hall. Practice, practice, practice!

Here are three exercises to practice the switch:
(1 to 3 = lip purse; 4 to 6 = tongue block)

Switch Exercise 1

3½   3   4   5   then back down   5   4   3   3½

Switch Exercise 2

3½   3   4   3½   3   2

Switch Exercise 3

2   3½   3   4   5+   6+

Here are five riffs to practice tongue blocking and lip pursing:
(1 to 3 = lip purse; 4 to 10 = tongue block)

Riff One
All tongue blocks
4 5 6+ 6+ 6+ 5 4 6+

Riff Two
All tongue blocks
4 5+ 6+ 5 5+ 4

Riff Three
All tongue blocks
6+ 7 8 8+ 9 9 8+ 8 7 6+

Riff Four

Lip Pursing	Tongue Blocking
2 3½ 3½ 2 1 2+ 2	5 4 5+ 4

Riff Five
Tongue Block all but the third hole
7 6+ 4 4+ 4 3½ 3 6+

Now let's do some exercises to practice tongue slapping. Be careful not to use too much air when you play the chord or you may run out of breath before you finish the exercise.

Exercise 1

Chord	Tongue Slap			Chord	Chord
1-4	4	1	2+	1-4	1-4
Chord	Tongue Slap			Chord	
1-4	4	1	2+	1-4	

Exercise 2

Chord	Tongue Slap		Chord	Tongue Slap		
1-4	5		1-4	5+	5	4

Highlights:

Tongue block single notes by placing the area just before the tip of the top of your tongue over three holes to the left of the hole you wish to play.

This area of the tongue is right where the tongue begins to narrow.

Tongue slapping is playing a four note chord before placing your tongue on the three notes to the left of the note you are playing.

Lip purse holes 1 to 3; Tongue block holes 4 to 10. The exception to this rule is that you lip purse the bends on holes 4 through 10.

You Tube

It is time for our next YouTube demonstration. This one will focus on tongue blocking. The video is entitled "Tim Gartland on Tongue Blocking the Harp". You can search by title.

Demonstration (Track 13 on MP3's):

> Tongue blocking the major scales
> Tongue slapping scales
> Switch exercises
> Tongue Blocking riffs
> Tongue slapping exercises

Chapter 14

Slip of the Tongue: Playing Octaves with Tongue Blocking

"Better the foot slip than the tongue."

- French Proverb

An octave is the same notes played at the same time, one higher or lower than the other on the scale. Think of a piano keyboard. If you play middle C, to the right of that note, 7 whole steps up, you will find another C, one with a higher pitch.

How to play octaves:

Place the area of the top of your tongue just before the tip (the area where the tongue begins to narrow) on the 2 and 3 holes. This is similar to tongue blocking one note only you are blocking two holes not three.

Blow the 1 and 4 holes through the left and right sides of your mouth. Feel the tongue on the 2 and 3 holes. Once again, be patient with your tongue. This is another new assignment for this muscle.

You should hear two notes with the same pitch only one is higher than the other.

Notice how full sounding the octave sounds, compared to playing a single note. Playing octaves will be a part of your growing arsenal of techniques that will make your solos more diversified and interesting.

Take a look at the diagram below; the blow notes have a consistent pattern all the way up the harp.

Blow Notes	A	C#	E	A	C#	E	A	C#	E	A
	1	2	3	4	5	6	7	8	9	10
Draw Notes	B	E	G#	B	D	F#	G#	B	D	F#

If you block the 2 and 3 blow and head up the harp maintaining this embouchure one hole at a time, you can play octaves all the way up from the 1-4+ octave to the 7-10+ octave.

Blow Octaves

1+-4+ A octave

2+-5+ C# octave

3+-6+ E octave

4+-7+ A octave

5+-8+ C# octave

6+-9+ E octave

7+-10+ A octave

Practice these octaves so that you can play them cleanly and smoothly all the way up the harp. As you travel up, make sure your lips and tongue are moist so that they do not stick to the harp. Move your head not your hands and make sure the embouchure stays intact for the whole trip. While you are doing this you will appreciate why another nickname for the harp is the licking stick! As always, check the MP3 recording to hear how this should sound.

Drawing Octaves:

With the 1 and 4 draw octave, like the 1 and 4 blow, you will block the 2 and 3 holes and you get a true octave.

After the 1-4 draw, two interesting things happen as you go up the harp with your draw octaves.

The 2-5 draw is not an octave, but is similar to a 7th chord. Seventh chords (with the flatted 7th blue note) are great for playing blues, rhythm and blues and rock. The two notes you are playing are the E and the D. The D is the minor 7th in the E scale and is a "blue" note.

1	2	3	4	5	6	7	8	9	10

Draw Notes B E G# B D F# G# B D F#

The second interesting thing occurs when you move up to the next hole. Check out the diagram above.

Notice you will need to block three holes for the remaining draw octaves on the harp (G#, B, D, F#). So, no surprise you need to open a little wider to block the three holes with your tongue to get the 3 and 7 octave, 4 and 8 octave, 5 and 9, and 6 and 10.

The three hole octave is yet another new task for your tongue. Promise your tongue this is the last of its new duties for a while and you will take it for ice cream after it masters the draw octaves.

1-4- B octave   2 hole

2-5- E7 octave   2 hole

3-7- G# octave   3 hole

4-8- B octave   3 hole

5-9- D octave   3 hole

6-10- F# octave   3 hole

Now try this scale exercise:

1+4+ octave   1-4- octave   2+5+ octave   2-5- octave   (then back down)

86

Also, experiment with combining tongue slapping and playing octaves by playing the chord before slapping the tongue on the octave.

1+-4+ Chord

1+-4+ Octave

1-4-   Chord

1-4-   Octave   Repeat exercise twice

****Muscle Memory Drill****

Tongue Thrust Drills: This drill will help you control the movement of your tongue for tongue blocking. With your mouth open enough to play four holes, start with your tongue in its relaxed position. Now move your tongue forward quickly into your mouth opening while exhaling. You will be making a slight whooshing sound.

Do three sets of 10 along with your other drills to help you warm up and develop your tongue dexterity.

Here are some riffs combining bent notes, individual notes and octaves:

Riff 1

	Octave					Octave		
4½ 4	2-5-		1	2+	2	2-5	2+5+	1-4

Riff 2

					Octave	
2	3½	3	4	5 +	3+	6+

Riff 3

Octave				Octave		
2-5-	2+5+	1-4	2	2-5-	2+5+	1-4-

Riff 4

		Octave		
2	3	1+4+	4	2

Riff 5

	All Octaves				
3+6+	3+6+	3-7-	4-8-	5+8+	6+9+

A nice exercise to practice the three hole blocks on the draw octaves is to go back and forth between the 6 and 9 blow (two hole block) and the 6 and 10 draw (three hole block).

6+9+ octave blow

6-10- octave draw

6+9+ octave blow

6-10- octave draw

Take some time with this so that you can do this cleanly. You will need to be well versed in switching between the two hole and three hole octaves. When you begin to solo up there, you must be able to quickly switch back and forth between the two.

Highlights:

The blow octaves are played by blocking the two middle holes with your tongue and playing the adjacent holes through the right and left side of your mouth.

The 1 and 4 draw octave is similar to the 1 and 4 blow, you block holes 2 and 3.

When you draw the 2 and 5 octave, you block holes 3 and 4 and you get a 7th chord.

Drawing octaves 3 through 10 require you block the three holes.

Demonstration (Track 14 on MP3's):

- ➢ Blow octaves
- ➢ Draw octaves
- ➢ 1+4 to 2-5- scale exercise
- ➢ Tongue slapping and octaves exercise
- ➢ Riffs
- ➢ 6+9+ blow and 6-10- draw and octave exercise

Chapter 15

Listening to Others:
My Harp Heroes

"We all have idols. Play like anyone you care about, but try to be yourself while you're doing so."

- B.B. King

They say "you are what you eat," and as musicians, we are what we listen to. Someone influences everybody. Listening to others is how we all develop and grow as players. Here are my favorite players.

Blues

I will limit my choices to two, with regrets to Junior Wells and Kim Wilson.

Little Walter:

No surprise here. It's like picking Babe Ruth as your favorite home run hitter. He has great tone, inventive playing, and excellent phrasing. He was inspired in part by the jazz and swing horn players of his day and you can hear it in his playing. You have to listen to some of his recordings if you want to play blues harp. Some of my all time favorite cuts are "Last Night," "Mellow Down Easy", and his solo behind Muddy Waters' "I Want You To Love Me."

Big Walter Horton:

Okay, I don't have a thing for the name Walter. This is also not a stretch as he is a giant among players. Tone is more his thing than flashy playing. I love his lush vibrato, and his ability to change his attack from sledgehammer to delicate as needed. What are my favorite recordings? Pick up his CD "Fine Cuts;" all the songs are outstanding. For classic tracks behind other players, his solos on "Walking By Myself" by Jimmy Rogers and Muddy's "Just to Be With You" slay me every time.

Folk

Bob Dylan:

His technique is limited by playing with a harp holder and the harp is his second instrument. When he does play he plays with passion and conviction. I like his playing on the songs "You Gonna Make Me Lonesome When You Go" and "Blowing in the Wind".

Rock and Roll
John Popper of the band Blues Traveler:

Any harp player who has played the national anthem at a World Series should not answer to anyone. He developed his own style of lightning fast playing and use of the upper register. He has brought the harp back on the radio waves with hits like "The Hook" and "Run Around".

Country
Mickey Raphael:

He is the harp behind Willie Nelson's records since the 70's. I admire his thoughtful complimentary playing behind Willie's voice as much as his solo playing. He plays to the song and its melody first and foremost, and then adds color beyond that if the song needs it. The entire "Star Dust" CD by Willie contains harp worth listening to and learning from.

Rhythm and Blues:
Stevie Wonder:

I am sure with his talent he could be the world's greatest bassoon player in about three days if he wanted. The fact is, whenever he has a harp in his hand, he's one of the best. Stevie primarily plays chromatic harp (larger harp where sharps and flats are played using a slide button on the side versus bending reeds). However, his high-end diatonic harp playing on "Boogie on Reggae Woman" is the best I've ever heard.

This is a wonderful charcoal drawing by my good friend Dennis Kempel of the late great Little Walter.

Slow motion machines are great tools to help you breakdown the audio performance of whomever you are listening to. They slow down any solo so that you can figure out exactly what they are playing and learn it in slow speed. There are also applications for this for smart phones.

Demonstration (Track 15 on MP3's):

➤ Harp Heroes comments

Please visit my website at timgartland.com. On my site you will find links to my music and videos.

Chapter 16

My Favorite Phrases: Playing Warbles

"The phrases that men hear or repeat continually end by
becoming convictions…"

- Johann Wolfgang von Goethe

The *warble* to a harp player is like a favorite phrase to a public speaker. The warble is used by virtually every player out there performing blues, rock, folk and country.

The warble, also known as a trill, is the rapid alternation of two adjacent tones. The warble is played on the harp by moving your head rapidly back and forth between two adjacent holes.

There are fast warbles and slow warbles, but the most important thing to remember is they are played rhythmically, in time to the beat of the music. Each note is played the same length and the speed/tempo is consistent.

Warbles can be played by tongue blocking or lip pursing. Learn how to do it both ways. They sound different so you can pick and choose which one you want based on what you want to say in the song. I prefer to lip purse my warbles.

Start with the 4 and 5 draw warble. Move your head back and forth while drawing in on the 4 and 5 holes. You use your head versus your hands because you can be more precise that way. Start slowly and focus on playing each note an equal length and playing it with same tempo.

Another key to the warble is to hit the right speed of the warble from the very start. There is no ramping up from slow to fast speed. You have to hit the ground running and maintain the same speed throughout the warble.

Finally, try to draw your air into your mouth and to the upper rear of your skull. This will warm up your tone by creating a large and deep resonating chamber for your warble.

Next let's play the 4-5 blow warble.

Let's move on to the 3-4 draw warble.

Now play them in succession giving equal time to each.

4-5 warble

4+5+ warble

3-4 warble

And back…

3-4 warble

4+5+ warble

4-5 warble

There are plenty more warble possibilities on the harp: 1-2 draw, 5-6 draw, 8-9 draw, 1-2 blow, and others. Have fun experimenting. A ton of great harp solos have a warble in some part of it. You can actually perform an entire solo with just warbles. *An essential tip is to alternate between the blow and draw warbles to replenish your air supply in your lungs.*

You can also play octave warbles. My favorite is the 1-4/2-5 octave warble. Start on the 1-4 octave and move your head back and forth between the two.

1-4/2-5-octave warble

****SPOTLIGHT****
Rhythm is king in music. Play with other musicians or to recordings. This will help you play with rhythm. When playing a song, if you make a mistake, forget it and keep up with the song.

Here is a song that features the warble. I also added note bends and octaves.

Warble Like That

Bar 1	Bar 2	Bar 3	Bar 4
4-5 warble	1 2+ 1 2 1 2+	4-5 warble	1 2+ 1 2 1 2+

Bar 5	Bar 6	Bar 7	Bar 8
4+5+ warble	3 4+ 4 3 2 1	4-5 warble	1 2+ 1 2 1

Bar 9	Bar 10
2 full 1 1-4 octave 1-4 octave	2 full 1 1+4+ octave 1+4+ octave

Bar 11	Bar 12
4-5 warble	1 2+ 2+ 1 1

Here's another song with chord rhythm and warbles.

Rhythm Your Warbles

Chord	Chord	Chord	Chord
Draw	Blow	Draw	Blow
2-3-4	1-2-3-4+	2-3-4	1-2-3-4+

Warble
4-5

Chord	Chord	Chord	Chord
Draw	Blow	Draw	Blow
2-3-4	1-2-3-4+	2-3-4	1-2-3-4+

Warble
3-4

You Tube

It is time for our next YouTube demonstration. This one will focus on warbles. The video is entitled "Tim Gartland on Playing Warbles". You can search by title.

Highlights:

Move your head back and forth not your hands.

Start slowly and focus on playing each note an equal length and playing it with same tempo.

Demonstration (Track 16 on MP3's):

> The songs *"Warble Like That" and "Rhythm Your Warbles"*
> 4-5 warble
> Tongue Block versus Lip pursed warbles
> 4-5, 4+5+ to 3-4 and back exercise
> 1-4 and 2-5 warble octave

FAQ: Why do you use your head and not your hands while warbling?

Answer: Control. You have more of it moving your head than hands.

If you are interested in booking me for a performance or a lesson, you can do either or both from my website, timgartland.com

Chapter 17

First Things First:
First Position Scales

"Every artist was first an amateur."
- Ralph Waldo Emerson

First position playing is when the song you are playing and the key of the harp are one in the same. Most of the songs we learned in the early chapters were performed in the first position.

Major Scales in the First Position

The major scale maintains a constant interval pattern of notes. From the first (or root note), there is 1 whole step, 1 whole step, one half step, 1 whole step, 1 whole step, 1 whole step, and one final half step.

The major scale for the key of C (piano's white keys) is: C-D-E-F-G-A-B-C

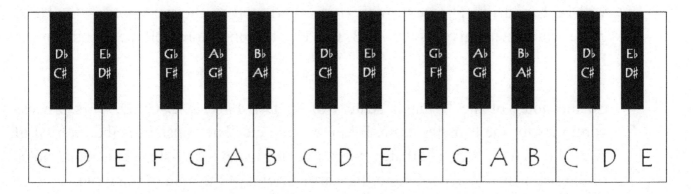

One piano key = a half step   Two piano keys = a whole step

In the diagram above, notice that between the C and D above is a black key, C# aka D♭. When you go one piano key up, from a C to a C# you have gone a half step. Because the first interval in a major scale is a whole step you must go up two piano keys. So the second note of the major scale has to be a D. Likewise, the next interval is a whole step so the next note must be an E. Since the next step is a half step, the next note is the F. Three more whole steps give us the G, A, and B notes. Finally, one more half step lands us back to a C, one octave higher.

Now for fun, let's figure out the notes of the major scale in the key of D. Remember, the major scale maintains a constant interval pattern of notes. That's two whole steps, then a half step, three more whole steps and one final half step.

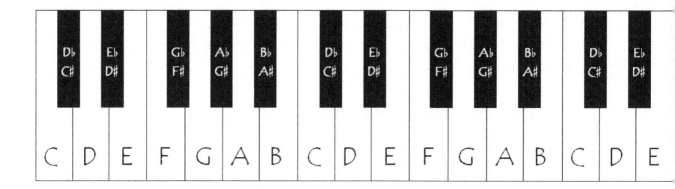

One piano key = a half step   Two piano keys = a whole step

From the D, we need to travel two separate whole steps, so the next two notes will be E and F#. The next interval is a half step so the next note is G. Three more whole steps give us the A, B, C#. Finally, one more half step lands on the D.

So the notes of the D major scale will be D-E-F#-G-A-B-C#-D. This process continues for the E major scale, F Major scale etc. The constant is the interval of two whole steps, then a half step, three full steps, and a half step. The actual notes of the scale change according to the starting point of the note of the scale.

The nice thing about the harmonica is that you don't need to memorize the notes of the major scale in all twelve keys. You need only memorize where the notes of the scale are found on the harp. When you play songs in different keys, you just change the key of the harp to match the song.

Since we are playing a harmonica in the key of A, we are going to play the A major scale. The easiest major scale to play is between the 4 and 7 holes. The 1 to 4 scale is more challenging. You have to hit your full/whole step bends on the 2 and 3 holes. With the third octave, the G# is only available if you can pull off a half note bend on the 10-hole.

Major Scale for harmonica in the Key of A

Full Note Bend										
Bent Blows										G#
Blow Notes	A	C#		A	C#	E	A	C#	E	A
	1	2	3	4	5	6	7	8	9	10
Draw Notes	B	E	G#	B	D	F#	G#	B	D	F#
Half Note Bends										
Full Note Bends		D	F#							
Full Note & a Half										

Three Octave Major Scale:

1+   1   2+   2full   2   3full   3

4+   4   5+   5   6+   6   7

7+   8   8+   9   9+   10   10½ +   10+   (then back down the scale)

Blues Scale in the First Position

Like the major scale, the blues scale has a specific interval of notes that remain constant no matter what key the scale is in. The interval for the blues scale is 1½ steps, 1step, ½ step, ½ step, 1½ steps and 1 step.

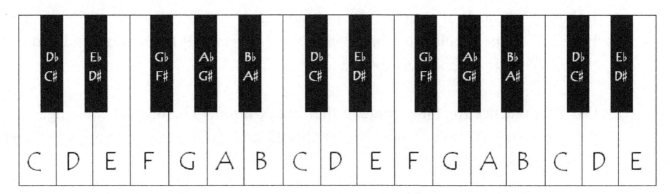

One piano key =a half step   Two piano keys = a whole step

106

Since we playing an A harp, and we are in the first position, let's figure out the blues scale in the key of A.

From the root note A, three piano keys or one and ½ steps bring you to the C. One step up from C is the D. A ½ step from D lands you on the D#. One more ½ step is the E. One and ½ steps from E is the G. One step from the G lands you back on an A that is an octave higher.

The blues scale in the key of A is: A-C-D-D#-E-G-A. Once again the interval of the blues scale are universal; the notes change based on what key the blues scale is in.

The blues scale is the major scale without a second note interval and with the third, fifth and seventh notes lowered a half step. The new scale produces a minor scale that sounds sadder, just plain bluesy.

A word about the blues scale in first position: it is quirkier than playing the blues in the second position. Holes 4 through 7 do not have any blue notes. As a result, you tend to play the blues in the first position on the 1 through 4 and 7 through 10 holes. When you do play holes 4 through 7, those notes are touchstones on your way to and from the lower and higher octaves.

In holes 1 through 4, the flatted 5th and 7th are available on the half note bends on the 2nd and 3rd holes (flatted 3rd is not available).

In holes 7 through 10, you hit the jackpot. All the blue notes are available. The flatted 3rd is the 8-hole blow bend, the flatted 5th is the 9-hole blow bend and the flatted 7th is the 10-hole full note bend.

Ok, let's practice the blues scale in the first position. The biggest challenges are the full and half note bends on the 2-hole and going from the 8-blow bend directly to the 9 draw.

The blues scale in A is A-C-D-D#-E-G-A. **The blue notes are C, D# and G** (flatted **3rd, 5th and 7th**). Because there is no flatted 3rd in the first and second octave, I have added the major third C# as touch stones.

	1	2	3	4	5	6	7	8	9	10
Full Note Bend										G
Half Note Bends								C	D#	
Blow Notes	A	C#		A	C#	E	A		E	A
	1	2	3	4	5	6	7	8	9	10
Draw Notes		E			D				D	
Half Note Bends		D#	G							
Full Note Bends		D								
Full Note & a Half										

The blues scale in A is A – C – D - D# - E – G - A.

Three Octave Blues Scale

1+   2+   2full 2½   2   3½

4+   5+   5   6+

7+   8+½   9   9+½ 9+   10+full   10+ (then back down the scale)

****SPOTLLIGHT****

Jimmy Reed, who had some big R&B hits in the 60's, popularized playing the blues in the 1st position. The high note bends were a big part of his sound. His songs include "Big Boss Man," "Bright Lights Big City" and "Hush Hush."

The Notes of the Twelve Bar Blues Progression

It is crucial when playing the 12 bar blues that you know where the root note holes are for the three chords in the progression. The root note is the same note value as the chord being played in the twelve bar pattern (example: playing an A note while the band is playing an A chord). For starters, playing this in a backing role behind a singer or soloist will allow you to play in tune with a band, and will in general, "do no harm." Let's take the harm out of harmonica shall we!

Here are the holes to play: (the first note is the I chord, the second the IV chord and the third note is the V chord)

Holes 1 through 4:   1+, 2full, 2
Holes 4 through 7:   4+, 5, and 6+
Holes 7 through 10: 7+, 9, and 9+

As long as you are in first position, these holes work for any song in any key!

Highlights:

In the first position the harp is played in the same key that the song is in.

The easiest major scale to play is between the 4 and 7 holes.

Blues Scales in First Position: 1 through 4 and 7 through 10 have the blue notes. You utilize 4 through 7 as touchstones on your way to and from the lower and higher octaves.

You Tube

It is time for our next You Tube demonstration. This one will focus on scales. The video is entitled "Tim Gartland on Playing the Major and Blues Scales". You can search by title.

Demonstration (Track 17 on MP3's):

➢ The major and blues scales

FAQ: What is the best harp key to play blues in the first position?

Answer: The key of A is my personal preference and the choice of a lot of harp players. I find that the bend notes in the upper register are easiest to play with the A harp. Also, there are a ton of blues and rock and roll songs in the key of A.

Chapter 18

Let Me Be the First to Say:
First Position Solos

"Get your facts first, and then you can distort them as much as you please."
- Mark Twain

Let's learn a couple of solos in the first position. The first is my interpretation of the piano solo in Chuck Berry's "Never Can Tell."

This was the song from the scene in the movie "Pulp Fiction" where John Travolta and Uma Thurman win the dance contest at the 50's retro diner "Jack Rabbit Slim's."

Never Can Tell
(On the MP3, the song is in C so I am playing a C harp)

2 3½ 3 4+ 3½ 3 2 3½ 2+ 2 1+ 2+

2 3½ 3 4+ 3½ 3 2 3½ 2+ 2 2½ 2full

2 3½ 3full 3 2 3½ 2+ 2 1 2 2½ 2full

2 3½ 3full 3 2 3½ 2+ 2 2 2+ 1+

1+4 Octave three times (as in Cha-Cha-Cha)

****SPOTLIGHT****

In the next song we will introduce a technique called the tongue flutter. The flutter is performed by rapidly and repeatedly placing and removing the tongue on and off the harp. Listen for it on the MP3's.

First Position Tongue Flutter Blues
(The song on the MP3 is in A, so I am using an A harp)

Bar 1   Bar 2

2   3½   3full   3full   2   3½   4+   4+   2   3½   3full   3full   2   3½   4+

Bar 3   Bar 4

1+4+Octave   1+4+Octave   3½   3full   2   2full   2+   1+   1+4+Octave

Bar 5

9+½   9+   9+   9   8+½   9+½   8+½   7+

Bar 6

9+½   9+   9+   9   8+½   9+½   8+½   7+

Bar 7   Bar 8

2   3½   4+   4+   3½   3½   2   2full   2+   1+   1+4+Octave

Bar 9

2full   2 full   1-4 octave tongue flutter

Bar 10

2full   2 full   1+ 4+ octave tongue flutter

Bar 11   Bar 12

2   3½   4+   4+   3½   3full   2   2full   2+   1+   1+4+octave tongue flutter

Demonstration (Track 18 on MP3's):

   ➢ The song "Never Can Tell"
   ➢ The song *First Position Tongue Flutter Blues*

Chapter 19

Plain Speaking Folks: Playing the Folk/Pop and Country Harp

"When you feel in your gut what you are and then dynamically pursue it - don't back down and don't give up - then you're going to mystify a lot of folks."

- Bob Dylan

In this chapter, we are going to learn the basics of playing Folk/Pop and Country harp. Folk and pop are played primarily in the first position. Beyond folk stars like Bob Dylan, Neil Young, Bruce Springsteen and scores of other artists play this style.

Folk/Pop harp most often focuses on playing the melody. Often the harp will take a short solo that closely follows the singer's melody line. In addition, the harp provides coloring of the song as only the harmonica can provide. Listen to songs, TV commercials, and movies and you can hear snippets of harmonica that add to the effect of the overall composition.

Folk/Pop relies mostly on the single note and chord approach with the occasional bend. Most of the folk pop artists rely exclusively on the pursed lips method versus the tongue blocking method.

Folk/Pop Harp

In addition to lip pursing, chords are also a part of this style. As you know to get the chord, open your mouth wider to hit the appropriate three or four notes that work over the chord progression of the song.

You will need to figure out the melody line of the song you are playing. If you are stuck, work with other musicians, or if you play another instrument, write it out and put it in harp notation.

When working with other musicians, share with them the layout of the notes on the harp (see the appendix at the end of this guide). That will provide a roadmap of the notes that are possible to play.

You do not have to play the melody line exactly. Due to the limitations of the harp in the first position, an abbreviated form of the melody line maybe the only option.

Here are my interpretations of a couple of famous Folk/Pop songs:

Promise Land by Bruce Springsteen

6+   6+ 6+ 6½ 6   6+ 6+ 6½ 6   6+ 6+   5+ 4+ 4 5+ 4 4+

6+   6+ 6+ 6½ 6   6+ 6+ 6½ 6   6+ 6+   5+ 4+ 4 5+ 4 4+

Heart of Gold by Neil Young

5+ 6+ 5 5+ 5 5+ 4+ 6+ 7+ 6 6+ 6 6+ 5+

5+ 5+ 5+ 6+ 6+ 6+ 5 5+ 5 5+ 4+

4+ 4+ 4+ 4+ 4+ 4+ 4+ 4   4+   3+

4+ 4+ 4+ 4+ 4+ 4+ 4+ 4   4+   3+

Country Harp

This style is played primarily in the second position. Like folk and pop harp, the emphasis is in supporting and embellishing the melody of the song. Unlike blues, most country songs are written using the major scale (versus the blues or minor scale).

Soloing is not as prevalent in country playing. If there is a solo, often it is just a half a chorus, often sharing the other half with a guitar, fiddle or piano.

A lot of country players use diatonic country tuned harps. The major difference is the 5 draw note which is a half step higher, a major 7th versus a minor 7th. This allows you to play a true major scale on holes 2 through 6 in the second position.

Here is my version of a classic country tune where the harp follows the songs melody.

Help Me Make it Through the Night by Kris Kristofferson

3full 3 4+ 3 3full 3 1   3full 3 4+ 3 3full 3 2+

3full 3 4+ 3 3full 3 2½ 4 4 3½ 3full 2   2+   2

Highlights:

You will need to figure out the melody line of the song you are playing.

The harp provides coloring of the song as only the harmonica can.

Folk/Pop harp relies on the single note approach, chords with the occasional bend.

Country Harp is played primarily in the second position, focuses on the melody and is based more on the major scale than the blues scale.

Demonstration (Track 19 on MP3's):

> ➤ *Promised Land*
> ➤ *Heart of Gold*
> ➤ *Help Me Make It through the Night*

I give lessons via the internet through services like Skype. For more information, visit my website at timgartland.com.

Chapter 20

I'll Second That:
Second Position Scales

"Always be a first-rate version of yourself, instead of a second-rate version of somebody else."

-Judy Garland

The second position is actually the first choice for the majority of harp players. *Second position harp is played with the harp four keys above the key the song is in.* So if the song is in E, the harp would be A. If the song is in G the harp is in C. And so on.

All three blue notes are available in the heart of the harp by playing the 3½, 4½ and 5draw. Elsewhere they are found on the 1½ draw, 2full, 9draw and 10+full.

First let's learn how to play the major scale in the second position using the A harp. The 7th note in the E major scale is D#. Here we have only the D, which is a minor 7th (a blue note). So, even when you try to play the major scale in the second position, it sounds bluesy.

Bent Blows										
Blow Notes				A	C#	E	A	C#	E	
	1	2	3	4	5	6	7	8	9	10
Draw Notes		E	G#	B	D	F#	G#	B	D	
Half Note Bends										
Full Note Bends			F#							
Full Note and a Half										

The major scale in the key of E is:

E-F#-G#-A–B-C#-D#-E.

The two octave major scale in second position is:

2   3full 3 4+ 4 5+ 5 6+ 6 7 7+ 8   8+ 9   9+ (then back down)

Ok, now let's learn to play the blues scale in the key of E. You noticed when playing the E major scale that the first note in the second position is the 2 draw versus the 1 or 4 blow we use in the first position. The same is true with the blues scale.

122

You are set up perfectly to play the blues scale in holes 2 through 6. In holes 6 through 9 you have one blue note, a flat 7th on the 9 draw.

The Blues Scale in the Key of E is:

E – G – A –A# – B – D – E. **The blue notes are G, A# and D.**

Once again, use lip pursing for 1 through 3 and tongue blocking for 4 through 10 (except for the 4 draw bend).

Half Note Bent Blows										
Blow Notes				A		E	A		E	
	1	2	3	4	5	6	7	8	9	10
Draw Notes		E		B	D		G#	B	D	
Half Note Bends			G	A#						
Full Note Bends										
Full Note & a Half										

The two octave blues scale in second position is:

2   3½   4+   4½   4   5   6+   7   7+   8   9   9+

I have highlighted other partial blues scale opportunities in holes 1 and 2 and holes 9 and 10. In holes 1 and 2, the 1 blow, 1 draw bend, 1 draw, 2 full draw bend, and 2 draw offer two thirds of a blues scale starting on the A-Bb-B-D and E (1 draw bend being the flat 5th and the 2 full note draw bend being the flat 7th.)

The 9 and 10 holes have half a blues scale with the 9 draw, 9 blow, 10 blow full note bend and 10 blow, or D-E-G-A (9 draw is the flat 7th and the 10 blow bend the flat 3rd.)

123

There are blue note opportunities all over the harp. When you are soloing, you are not going to just play the straight octave scale. You will be improvising, jumping to different places on the harp while building your solo. You need to know where all the blue notes are in all ten holes as well as the root notes of the twelve bar form. The blues scale contains six distinct notes. Imagine before you the numbers 1 through 6. How many different numbers could you create by mixing up the sequence? The same is true with using the scales and mixing up the notes and rhythms to create new and unique solos.

Full Note Bends										**G**
Half Note Bends										
Blow Notes	A			A		E	A		E	A
	1	2	3	4	5	6	7	8	9	10
Draw Notes	B	E		B	D		G#	B	D	
Half Note Bends	A#		G	A#						
Full Note Bends		D								
Full Note & a Half										

Partial Blues Scales in the 1, 2, 9 and 10 holes:

1+   1½   1   2full   2   9   9+   10+full   10+

Playing blues scales in holes 1 through 10:

1+   1½   1   2full   2   3½   4+   4½   4   5   6+   7   7+   8   9   9+

10+full   10+

Remember what key the scale is in:
Scales begin and end on the note of the key the scale is in. If you play the blue scales in holes 1 through 10 above, the first and last note would be an A (with an A harp). You are actually playing the blues scale in the key of E. To help you remember what key you are in, when you begin and end playing the blues scales in holes 1 to 10, begin and end with the 2 draw, which is an E. (see next page)

Blues scales in holes 1 through 10 beginning and ending with 2 draw:

2   1+   1½   1   2full   2   3½   4+   4½   4   5   6+   7   7+   8   9   9+

10+full   10+   (then back down scale)

The Notes of the Twelve Bar Blues Progression

It is crucial when playing the 12 bar blues that you know where the root note holes are for the three chords in the progression. The root note is the same note value as the chord being played in the twelve bar pattern (example: playing an A note while the band is playing an A chord). For starters, playing this in a backing role behind a singer or soloist will allow you to play in tune with a band, and will in general, "do no harm."

Here are the holes to play: (the first note is the I chord, the second the IV chord and the third note is the V chord)

Holes 1 through 4:   2, 4+, 4
Holes 4 through 8:   6+, 7+, 8

Again, as long as you are in second position, these holes work for any song in any key!

Highlight:

Second position harp, or cross-position, is played with the harp four keys above the key the song is in. So if the song is in E, the harp would be A.

Demonstration (Track 20 on MP3's):

- ➢ The major scales
- ➢ The blues scales
- ➢ Partial blues scales

Important Advice

So far, we have introduced the major and minor scales in the first and second positions. I play these scales almost everyday and you should too! Commit these scales to memory. Specifically, the scales I want you to memorize are:

1) The Three Octave Major Scale in first position on page 106.
2) The Three Octave Blues Scale in first position on page 108.
3) The Two Octave Major Scale in second position on page 122.
4) Blues scales in second position in holes 1 through 10 beginning and ending with 2 draw on page 125.

Three Octave Major Scale in First Position:
1+ 1 2+ 2full 2 3full 3 4+ 4 5+ 5 6+ 6 7
7+ 8 8+ 9 9+ 10 10½+ 10+ (then back down)

Three Octave Blues Scale in First Position:
1+ 2+ 2full 2½ 2 3½ 4+ 5+ 5 6+
7+ 8+½ 9 9+½ 9+ 10+full 10+ (then back down)

The Two Octave Major Scale in Second Position:
2 3full 3 4+ 4 5+ 5 6+ 6 7 7+ 8 8+ 9 9+ (then back down)

Blues Scales in Second Position beginning and ending with 2 draw:
2 1+ 1½ 1 2full 2 3½ 4+ 4½ 4 5 6+ 7 7+ 8 9 9+
10+full 10+   (then back down)

Later in the book we will add one more position and scale for you to play everyday. That will be the Third Position Blues Scale (Playing blues scales in holes 1 through 10 beginning and ending with 1 draw, page 157).

Blues Scales in Third Position beginning and ending with 1 draw:
1 1+ 1 2full 2 3full½ 3full 4+ 4 5 6+ 6½ 6 7+ 8 9 9+ 10 10+
(then back down)

Chapter 21

Do You Have a Second?: Second Position Solo

"In this world second thoughts, it seems, are best."

- Euripides

We are going to play a solo in the second position. I wrote this solo using as much of the harp as I could so you can practice playing the whole instrument. In addition, I added octaves and a warble as well. I threw in everything but the kitchen sink.

This song is not easy to play. You are probably not going to "own it" in one sitting. It is best to break it into sections and try to master a section at a time.

The Kitchen Sink Blues

Bars 1 through 4

2   3   4   5+   2-5octave   2+5+octave   1-4octave   1+4+octave

2-5octave   2+5+octave   1-4octave   1+4+octave   3½   3+6+octave

3+6+octave   3+6+octave

Bars 5 and 6

1+   2+   2   3½   4+   4   3½   2

Bars 7 and Bar 8

4½   4   4½   4   5   6+   6+

Bar 9

8   9   8   8+   9   8

Bar 10

9   8+8   7   6   6+   5+   6+

Bars 11 and Bar 12

4-5warble   3½   3full   2   2full   2

Demonstration (Track 21 on MP3's):

  ➢ Song Demonstration *The Kitchen Sink Blues*

Chapter 22

Talkin' 'Bout the Blues: Blues Harp Playing

"I had the blues because I had no shoes until upon the street, I met a man with no feet."

- Anonymous

There is no music more American than the blues. Let's talk about playing the blues on one of its premier instruments, the harp.

You cannot play good blues, or any music for that matter, without an emotional connection to the music. Sure, you need the technical skills to play blues harp, but that is not enough to reach an audience. You have to feel the piece you are playing. Listen to the lyrics, listen to the rhythm, become part of the message the song is conveying.

If you master the blues scales in all three positions (third position playing will be covered in chapters 28 and 29) you are on your way. Using your own creativity in how you interpret the song, you will put your stamp on any song you play.

Playing the blues is not about achieving technical perfection. Blues great Willie Dixon (bassist, song writer, and producer) would insist that his records have at least one mistake. There is something inorganic and clinical about blues that is played too perfectly.

Having said that, you still want to play with proficiency, but you have to play with emotion as well.

When recording, I often use the first take because it's the freshest and most exciting, even if there are a few mistakes. However, I do prepare for my recordings and have a general idea of where I want the solo to go before the record button is pushed.

The lyrics and the melody line can provide you with the basis of what you want to say in your solo. Make sure what you are playing is carrying the song forward, and that it fits with the mood and vibe of the song.

Here's an example of what I am talking about. Below is my interpretation of a single verse solo of Little Walter's slow blues "Last Night." This solo is a great example of restraint, playing only what is needed to make the song better. Walter does this song in the key of D playing in the second position with a G harp, but we can do it in the key of E with an A harp.

Last Night

Bar 1	Bar 2	Bar 3
4 and 5 draw warble	4 and 5 draw warble	4 and 5 draw warble

Bar 4

3 4+ 4 5+ 5 5+ 4 3½ 3full 2 2full 2+ 1+

Bar 5	Bar 6
1+4+ octave tongue flutter	4 4½ 3 2 1+4+ octave tongue flutter

Bar 7	Bar 8
2 3 4+ 4½ 4 and 5 warble	4 and 5 warble

Bar 9	Bar 10
4½ 4 4½ 4+ 3 4 3 2 2	2 3½ 4+ 4 3 2

Bar 11   Bar 12

2full 1 1½   1   2   4 and 5 warble 2 2full 1 1 2 2full 1   2

131

Soling 101: A classic approach is to start simple, perhaps with the lower notes, play more rhythmic parts, perhaps a warble. As the solo continues, you would build the intensity by playing faster runs and finishing playing the higher notes of the harp. Other songs may call for a simple interpretation of the melody line. Sometimes holding just one note over a section of the solo can build drama that the song can benefit from.

Demonstration (Track 22 on MP3's):

➤ The solo from "Last Night"

FAQ: What's the greatest blues harp solo of all time?

Answer: Of course this is a ridiculously subjective question, but I choose Junior Well's solo on "Hoodoo Man Blues" from the album of the same name. It is played with the same emotion and feeling conveyed in the music and lyrics of the song.

Chapter 23

Good Vibrations:
Playing with Vibrato

"We vibrate, our hearts are pumping blood; we are a rhythm
machine, that's what we are."

- Mickey Hart

In this chapter we introduce how to play with *vibrato*, which is an essential technique for any harp player who wants to climb up on stage. *Vibrato is defined as a small fluctuation of pitch used as an expressive device to intensify the sound.*

Playing With Vibrato

The next tool for your musical toolbox is playing with vibrato. Specifically, we will learn throat vibrato, versus the similar effects that can be done with your hands. This becomes particularly important when you are playing with a handheld microphone since your hands are otherwise occupied.

Trust me, after you have been playing for a while you will play with vibrato without even thinking about it. If you have ever had a cough, then your throat muscles have performed the action necessary to play the harp with vibrato.

Without the harp, cough, using only a small fraction of the air normally associated with the action, almost like you were really physically weak or trying to cough very, very, quietly. You want to cough over and over again in this way and develop a steady rhythm. Like the warble, it is important that you maintain the speed of your vibrato.

The sound and the rhythm to me are reminiscent of a quiet version of the machine gun sound kids from my neighborhood made back in the day.

Now play the 4 blow simulating this throat action. Make sure the vibrato is played in a steady rhythm. Experiment with separate vibratos using slower and faster tempos.

Now try this on the 4 draw. The throat action is the same only now you are drawing in air. You may find the draw vibrato requires a little more concentration. It's kind of like a reverse cough. It is a bit unnatural since you are drawing in air versus blowing out when you cough normally.

Try your vibrato on the last line of the National Anthem "...and the home of the brave."

4+   4   5+   5   4   4+

Vibrato with Bends

One of the most expressive sounds you can make with the harp is adding vibrato to a note bend. The best place to start is the 4 draw. Play the 4 draw, and then bend the 4 draw. Now add your vibrato.

Trying these exercises will help you to control the switch from normal playing to vibrato and also playing with vibrato on bent notes.

Exercise 1

4 draw without vibrato

4 draw with vibrato

41/2 draw bend without vibrato

41/2 draw bend with vibrato

Exercise 2

3 draw without vibrato

3 draw with vibrato

31/2 draw bend without vibrato

31/2 draw bend with vibrato

Exercise 3

2 draw without vibrato

2 draw with vibrato

2 full bend draw bend without vibrato

2 full bend draw bend with vibrato

If you can do this with control, you are well on your way to becoming a good harp player.

Now try this riff which is a great example of how cool the bend note with vibrato can sound:

2   3½ with vibrato   2

Highlights:

Without the harp, cough using only a small fraction of the air normally associated with the action.

Cough over and over again in this way and develop a steady rhythm.

The draw vibration requires more concentration since it is similar to a reverse cough which is less natural.

You Tube

It is time for our next You Tube demonstration. This one will be on vibrato. The video is entitled "Tim Gartland on Vibrato on the Harp". You can search by title.

Demonstration (Track 23 on MP3's):

> ➢ The sound of the vibrato action without the harp
> ➢ National Anthem
> ➢ The vibrato exercises
> ➢ Riff featuring bent note vibrato

Chapter 24

Something to Say:
20 Riffs for Solos and Practicing

"Quickly, bring me a beaker of wine, so that I may wet my
mind and say something clever."

- Aristophanes

When you are playing your harp, you need to have something to say. Here are 20 of my favorite riffs, some from well-known songs. These riffs are played in the second position.

The purpose is to add to your musical vocabulary. It can also serve as a guide for future practice sessions and as a way to warm up before a performance. Part of the inspiration for this chapter was an instructional book I had when I was learning. It had a section of cool riffs that I would often refer to when I was practicing.

Riffs are like building blocks for your solo playing. The 20 below are just a fraction of the possibilities. I made sure to include octaves, warbles, tongue blocks, half and full note bends, and cover the whole harp. *I also added some triplets, which are three notes played rapidly over just a single beat.*

20 Riffs
(Lip purse holes 1 through 3; tongue block 4 through 10, except for bends)

Riff 1
1 2full 2 3½ 2 2full 2full 2

Riff 2
1 2 3 4½ 4 4+ 4 3½ 2

Riff 3
2-5octave (3 times) 3+6+octave   2-5octave   3½   2

Riff 4
4 and 5 warble 4½   4

Riff 5
1 2+ 3 3½ 3   3 3½ 3

Riff 6

6+ 5 4+ 4 3½ 6+

Riff 7

7 6 6+ 4 4+ 3

Riff 8

2full 2½ 2 2   2full 2 full 2

Riff 9

6+ 7 8 8+ 9+½ 9

Riff 10

4½ 4 2/5 and 3/6 octave warble 2

Riff 11

2-5octave 2+5+octave 1-4octave 2 2-5octave 2+5+octave 1-4octave

Riff 12

2 3   2 3½   2 3full   2

Riff 13

6+ 5 4 4½ 4+ 3½ 2 2full 2

Riff 14

2 3 4 5 5 5+ 4 6+ (Quarter bend on first 5)

Riff 15 (triplet riffs)

4½ 4 5,   4½ 4 5,   4½ 4 5,   4+ 3½ 2

Riff 16

1-4octave 2-5octave 3+6+octave 3-7octave 3+6+octave

Riff 17

4-5 warble   4+ 5+ warble   3-4 warble   4+ 5+ warble   4-5 warble

Riff 18

6+ 6+ 7 8   8+   9+

Riff 19

9+ 9 8 7 6 6+ 5+   6+

Riff 20

9+1/2   9+   10+   10+full

****SPOTLIGHT****

When playing the 5 draw, you can bend it, but not to a true half note bend. Some call it a quarter note bend. It is sort of like when a guitar player bends a string up or down to the note he wants to pay. It is a cool effect and fairly easy to do. Listen for it on the MP3 on riff 14.

Highlights:

By practicing these riffs you will add to your musical vocabulary.

It can also serve as a guide for future practice sessions

Demonstration (Track 24 on MP3's):

> ➢ Play the riffs

This is a picture of myself with one of the giants on the harp, Mr. James Cotton.
(Boston, Massachusetts, 2011)

Chapter 25

Chorus of One:
Chord Playing

"There in the chords and the melodies, is everything I want to say"

- David Bowie

Chord playing was one of the original intentions for the instrument. The great versatility of the harp is that you can play melodies and chords very easily.

Chords are usually made up of three notes. The A major chord is A-C#-E.

You can see the first three blow notes on a harp in the key of A are A-C#-E, the A major chord. The same chord is found on the 4, 5, and 6 blow holes as well as the 7, 8, and 9 blow holes. When you are playing the ten hole diatonic harp, it is impossible to *not* play a version of the major chord when blowing out while hitting multiple notes.

Normal Notes	A	C#	E	A	C#	E	A	C#	E	A
	1	2	3	4	5	6	7	8	9	10
Normal Notes	B	E	G#	B	D	F#	G#	B	D	F#

In the first position, you can play the melody and inset the A major chord whenever the song starts or lands back on the root chord (A major). Here are some other chords available on the A harp.

B minor: B, D and F#: 4, 5 and 6 draw and 8, 9, and 10 draw.
E major: E, G# and B: 2, 3 and 4 draw
D major: Not all three notes, but the first two, D and F#, 5 and 6 draw, 9 and 10 draw

When playing in the second position, you need to know where the chords that make up the blues progression are (E, A and B using an A harp).

E Chord (E-G#-B)
2-3-4 draw

A Chord (A-C#-E)
4-5-6 blow

B minor chord (B-D-F#)*
4-5-6 draw

144

*You don't have a major chord, but you do have a minor, which works in a blues progression just fine.

Here's a simple chord based blues using the above:

Blues On Its Own Accord

2-3-4 draw for 4 bars

4-5-6+ blow for 2 bars

2-3-4 draw for 2 bars

4-5-6 draw for 1 bar

4-5-6+ blow for 1 bar

2-3-4 draw for 1 bar

4-5-6 draw for 1 bar

Highlights:

The harp was designed to play chords and melodies

Chords are usually made up of the three notes.

It is pretty hard not to land on a major chord when you are blowing out.

Demonstration (Track 25 on MP3's):

> ➤ Playing the blues progression chords
> ➤ Playing the song "Blues On Its Own Accord"

Chapter 26

Striking the Right Chord: Chord Songs

"I don't think when I play…when I am playing the right chords appear in my mind like photographs…"

- Earl "Fatha" Hines

Playing the right chords and notes without thinking will come to you over time. Ironically, effortless playing requires a great deal of effort in the form of practice and preparation. So on that note, here is some music for you to play. It shows you what you can do with chords on the harp. Grab your C harp for the next two songs.

Little Drummer Boy

4+-6+ Chord   4+-6+ Chord   4   5+   5+   5+   5+   5   5+   5   5+7+ Chords

4+6+ Chord   4+6+ Chord   4   5+   5+   5+   5+   5   5+   5   5+7+ Chords

4   4   5+   5   5   5   6   6+   5   5+   4

4   4   5+   5   5   5   6   6+   5   5+   4   6+ 5 5+ 4   6+ 5 5+ 4

4+6+ Chord   4+6+ Chord   4   5+   5+   5+   5+   5   5+   5   5+7+ Chords

4   4+   4   4+6 Chord

148

Blues According to You

(This song is in G, you have a C harp so you are playing in the second position).

G Chord Bars 1 and 2
2-4 Chord   2-4 Chord   2-4 Chord   2-4 Chord,   2+ 1   2   2+   1   2
2-4 Chord   2-4 Chord

G Chord Bars 3 and 4
2-4 Chord   2-4 Chord   2-4 Chord   2-4 Chord   2+   1   2   2+   1   2
2-4 Chord   2-4 Chord

C Chord Bars 5 and 6
4+6+ Chord   4+6+ Chord   4+6+ Chord   4+6+ Chord   3   2   4+6+ Chord   3
2   4+6+ Chord   4-6+ Chord   4-6+ Chord

G Chord Bars 7 and 8
2-4 Chord   2-4 Chord   2-4 Chord   2-4 Chord   2+   1   2   2+   1   2
2-4 Chord   2-4 Chord

D Chord Bar 9
4-6 Chord   4-6 Chord   4-6 Chord   4-6 Chord
4-6 Chord   4-6 Chord   4-6 Chord   4-6 Chord

C Chord Bar 10
 4-6+ Chord   4-6+ Chord   4-6+ Chord   4-6+ Chord
4-6+ Chord   4-6+ Chord   4-6+ Chord   4-6+ Chord

G Chord   Bar 11   D Chord Bar 12
2-4 Chord   2+   1   2-4 Chord   2+   1   2-4Chord   1   1

Demonstration (Track 26 on MP3's):

> ➤ "Little Drummer Boy"
> ➤ "Blues According to You"

149

For the latest news on all my musical activities, please visit my website at timgartland.com.

Chapter 27

Hands Free Communication:
Playing Harp with a Holder

"Look Mom… no hands!"

Countless numbers of kids freaking out their mothers

Playing with a harp holder frees your hands to accompany yourself if you play another instrument. This can really add color to your live performances. Sometimes a little harp goes a long way, especially if you are doing a solo or duo gig.

Setting up the holder's position is the key for getting comfortable with playing with one. Here are some tips to adjusting your holder.

First, place the neck portion of the holder inside the collar of your shirt (if you're wearing a shirt with a collar). This will help stabilize the harp so it does not move around as much.

Next, adjust the harp in the holder so that it sticks out as much as possible while still being firmly fixed. When you go to play, you want as much harp available as you can.

Now adjust the wing nuts so that the angle is comfortable for you to play. Make sure they are tight so that the arm of the rack does not move when you are playing.

If you are going to sing, make sure you can pull your head back from the rack and sing comfortably in the microphone.

****SPOTLIGHT****

Playing the harp with the holder is more difficult than playing with your hands. Try it out and you will have an appreciation for how important your hands are in playing harp, not only for tone control, but also simple control of your instrument. It is like trying to eat a hot dog without using your hands.

It really is not possible for you to be as precise with rack playing as with your hands. But it is this lack of precision that is part of the appeal of this sound. At a minimum, you are adding color or texture to your music that only the harp can bring.

Here some additional tips for playing with a rack:

You can play in any position, but first position is the most popular and easiest.

I like to play the melody, usually in the 4 to 7 holes in the first position.

Playing chords on the harp supporting what you are playing on your other instrument sound cool as well.

Second position involves bending notes, which of course is a little bit more difficult, but doable.

You can use tongue blocking or the pursed lips method, but pursed lips is simpler and the method that is used most frequently.

Highlights:

Place the neck portion of the holder inside the collar of your shirt if you are wearing one.

Adjust the harp in the holder so that it sticks out as much as possible. When you go to reach for it, you want as much harp available as you can.

You can play in any position, but first position is the most popular and easiest

Demonstration (Track 27 on MP3's):
> ➢ I play a song with guitar and rack harp

If you are interested in lessons, visit my website at timgartland.com

Chapter 28

Third Time's a Charm: Third Position Scales

"Life is a moderately good play with a badly written third act."

- Truman Capote

The *third position* is a lesser-utilized harp position that will reward you with a different sound alternative than the first and second.

The third position is much better suited for playing the blues scale than the major scale So much so that I am going to forego teaching you the major scale in the third position (however, you can hear it on the MP3). Grab your A harp and let's get to work on this.

Since you have an A harp, and the third position scales starts on the 1 draw, the blues scale will be in the key of B. The blues scale in the key of B is: B – D – E – F – F# – A – B. **The blue notes are D, F and A.** You have two complete blues scales in holes 1 through 8. This is far better than both first and second position.

Holes 1 through 4 provide the flatted 3rd with the full note bend on the 2 draw, flatted 5th with full½ note bend on the 3 draw and the flatted 7th with the 4 blow. In holes 4 through 8, 5 draw is the flat 3rd, the 6½ draw bend is the flatted 5th and the 7 blow is the flatted 7th.

	1	2	3	4	5	6	7	8	9	10
Full Note Bends										
Half Note Bends										
Blow Notes				A		E	A			
	1	2	3	4	5	6	7	8	9	10
Draw Notes	B	E		B	D	F#		B		
Half Note Bends						F				
Full Note Bends		D	F#							
Full Note & a Half			F							

The blues scale in the key of B is: B- D - E - F – F#- A - B.

The two-octave blues scale in third position is:

1   2full   2   3full½   3full   4+   4   5   6+   6½   6   7+   8

Expanding our view beyond the two octaves to all ten holes, the third position offers the most blue notes of any position (nine). The first position has five blue notes. The second position has seven blue notes

The 1 blow gives you the flatted 7th and the 9 and 10 holes give you a partial blues scale with the flatted 3rd with the 9 draw and the flatted 7th with the 10 blow.

Full Note Bends										
Half Note Bends										
Blow Notes	**A**			**A**		**E**	**A**		**E**	**A**
	1	2	3	4	5	6	7	8	9	10
Draw Notes	B	E		B	D	F#		B	D	F#
Half Note Bends						**F**				
Full Note Bends		**D**	F#							
Full Note and a Half			**F**							

Playing the blues scale in holes 1 through 10:

1+ 1   2full   2 3full½ 3full 4+   4   5   6+   6½   6   7+ 8 9 9+ 10 10+

Remember what key the scale is in:
Scales begin and end on the note of the key the scale is in. If you play the blue scales in holes 1 through 10 above, the first and last note would be an A (with an A harp). You are actually playing the blues scale in the key of B. To help you remember what key you are in, when you begin and end playing the blues scales in holes 1 to 10, begin and end with the 1 draw, which is a B.

Playing blues scales in holes 1 through 10 beginning and ending with 1 draw:

1 1+ 1   2full   2 3full½ 3full 4+   4   5   6+   6½   6   7+ 8 9 9+ 10 10+
(then back down)

157

The Notes of the Twelve Bar Blues Progression

It is crucial when playing the 12 bar blues that you know where the root note holes are for the three chords in the progression. The root note is the same note value as the chord being played in the twelve bar pattern (example: playing an A note while the band is playing an A chord).

Here are the holes to play: (the first note is the I chord, the second the IV chord and the third note is the V chord)

Holes 1 through 4:   1, 2, 3full
Holes 4 through 8:   4, 6+, 6
Hole 8 through 10:   8, 9+, 10

Again, as long as you are in third position, these holes work for any song in any key.

Highlights:

Third position is played with the harp one key lower than the key the song is in.

The first note of the third position scale is the 1 draw (B).

Third position is ideal for playing blues because of all the blue note possibilities.

Demonstration (Track 28 on MP3's):

> ➢ Blue scale
> ➢ Partial Blues Scale

Chapter 29

Three to Get Ready: Third Position Solo

"By three methods do we learn wisdom: first by reflection, which is the noblest; second by imitation, which is the easiest; and third, by experience, which is the most bitter."

- Confucius

Let's learn a solo in the third position. This solo is one I performed on the recording of the Porch Rockers' version of "Snatch It Back and Hold It" off their Covers CD. On the recording the band was in A so I used a G harp. Here we will do it in the key of B using our A harp.

Snatch It Back and Hold It
First Verse:
Bar 1   Bar 2
4 and 5 warble   4½ 4 5 5+ 4 5+

Bar 3   Bar 4
4 5 6+ 5 6   6+   5 6+ 5 4   4 4+3 4+ 3 4+ 4

Bar 5   Bar 6   Bar 7   Bar 8
1 2full 2 2   2full 1   1 2 full 2 2   2full 1

Bar 9   Bar 10
4 and 5 played together no tongue   4 and 5 played together no tongue

Bar 11   Bar 12
4 and 5 warble   4 and 5 warble

Second Verse:
Bar 1   Bar 2   Bar 3   Bar 4
9 9 8+ 8 9 8+ 8 8+   9 9 8+ 8 9   8+ 8 8+

Bar 5   Bar 6   Bar 7   Bar 8
8 9 9+ 9 10 9+9 9+ 9   8+ 9 8+ 8   8+ 8 7 8-9

Bar 9   Bar 10   Bar 11   Bar 12
4 5 4   4 5 4   4 and 5 warble   4 and 5 warble

Demonstration (Track 29 on MP3's):

➢ Solo from Snatch It back and Hold It

160

Chapter 30

Somebody Hand Me the Microphone: Microphones for Harp Playing

"This mic is a b**** Leonard."

- Recorded studio banter of Little Walter yelling at Leonard Chess (Chess Records) about his microphone during a recording session.

161

If that Little Walter quote didn't convey the passion harp players have for the right microphone, nothing will.

There are several microphones favored by harp players to achieve certain sounds or tones. The choice of a microphone or mic depends on what style of music you are playing and what you are trying to say musically.

Microphones for playing Acoustic Harp

If you want your harp to sound as natural as possible, you should use microphones that vocalist use.

Playing acoustic harp in a band setting involves using a quality vocal mic through a public address system (PA).

I like the *Shure SM58 microphone*. This is a very popular mic and available at most music stores.

To play acoustically, hold the harp like normal and place it in close proximity to the mic. I like to have the outside of my hands just touching the outside of the mic. Avoid cupping the mic as this will cause feedback discussed later in the chapter. You can change the volume and the sound by cupping and un-cupping your hands and using the wah-wah and fanning techniques.

Microphones for Amplified Playing

These are also known as *bullet microphones* because of their shape. They are normally plugged into a guitar amplifier.

These mics change the natural tone of the harp to make them sound more electric. It is similar to the difference between the sounds of an acoustic guitar versus an electric guitar.

The *Astatic JT-30*, also known as the *Blues Blaster* and other names, is a favorite of many harp players. The JT-30 has a warm sound. Combined with the right amp, the sound created becomes muscular, more like a saxophone than the acoustic harp.

The *Shure Green Bullet* has more of an edgy, mid-range tone the works best for rock and roll and rhythm and blues.

I own both of these mics. They do different things and I like having both available depending on what the song requires. They are available in stock or can be ordered by most music stores.

For both of these mics, grip the harp like normal and place the bullet mic in the opening between your hands. The harp, mic and hands should act as one unit. You should create a near air-tight seal with your hands. This will create a focused, full, well-rounded sound that fits in perfectly with an electric band.

Be careful not to squeeze the harp mic to hard. This can fatigue your hands and arms over a night of playing.

Microphone feedback is that high pitched, irritating sound you hear from time to time during a live performance. If you are careful and have the right equipment, you shouldn't cause feedback.

The first step is testing your equipment and determining the feedback level at home before you play in public. This will allow you to find out how far you can go before that point of sonic "no return".

If you are playing acoustically, find the feedback level of the PA system and turn the volume level down a little.

If you are playing amplified, make sure you have a separate volume control on the bullet mic itself. This literally gives you fingertip control of your volume.

You Tube

It is time for our next YouTube demonstration. This one will demonstrate using microphones. The video is entitled "Tim Gartland on Harp Mics". You can search by title.

****SPOTLIGHT****

I have to admit that I was the cause of several feedback episodes during my early days of playing. It almost cost me a job with my first band. At the time, I did not have a bullet mic with a volume control. Now, I don't play a gig without one. I can't remember the last time I caused feedback.

Highlights:

To capture the natural sound of the harp, use a quality vocal mike through the PA system.

The Astatic JT-30/Blues Blaster has an electric sound with a warm muscular tone.

The Shure Green Bullet has an electric sound with an edgy, mid-range tone that works best for rock and roll and rhythm and blues

Demonstration (Track 30 on MP3's):

> Demonstrate each mic

FAQ: Do I have a mic preference?

Answer: No.

Currently, I do use the Astatic JT-30 more often than I use the other mics.

In the past, I played with a band with a rock and roll vibe so I used a green bullet with those guys.

Once again, the songs, the sound of the band will determine which mic works for you in any given situation.

Picture above are the Shure "Green Bullet", a Shure vocal microphone, and the Astatic JT-30.

Chapter 31

Speak Up:
Amplifiers for Harp Playing

"Why did they keep changing guitars and amplifiers when they were perfect?"

- Buddy Guy

When you are playing in a band, you've got to be heard. Plugging in to an amp will allow you to be heard when it's your time to "speak".

Sometime in the 1940's harp players began picking up mics and plugging in. The sound of the harp became more like a saxophone than an acoustic harp.

If you are just starting out, there is a good sounding amplifier from Fender called the Blues Junior that is relatively inexpensive.

Now I am going to talk about three of my favorite harp amps.

1965 Fender Super Reverb

This is a big boy; it weighs 65 pounds.

It has four 10" inch speakers so it is very loud.

I use this for big rooms or outdoor gigs were I am playing more rock stuff.

You know in fancy restaurants, where they match wines with entrees? I like matching the Shure Green Bullet with this amp.

For amplifier tone settings, I like the bass on 8, the middle or mid-range on 4, and the treble or high frequency on 4. These setting may need to be tweaked based on the acoustics of the venue.

You should set the reverb setting to suit your own taste. I set it between 2 and 3. Too much of a good thing is, well, too much.

This combination, the Green Bullet and the Super Reverb is excellent. But you have to make sure that it fits with the music you are playing. You will be well armed to compete with screaming guitars, rolling piano, and a rocking rhythm section.

I have an original 1965 Super Reverb Amplifier. Fender has re-issued this amp according to its original specifications.

1962 Fender Princeton

This is a small amp with a big sound. It is perfect for small rooms or recording. It has one 10" speaker. It weighs about 15 pounds. I like to match the Astatic JT-30 for this amp. It has a very warm sound, easy on the ears for listeners in a small club.

I boost the bass of any amp when playing harp. The boost works well with the harp, giving it a big tone. In the case of this amp, it only has one tone setting, which I set to around 2, 1 being the setting with the most bass.

The Princeton does not come with reverb. I use a Boss digital delay foot pedal designed for guitarists and available at most music stores. Once again don't overdue the delay effect.

Since this is a small amp, you may want to mic it and put it through the PA system. This will ensure that everyone in the room can hear you.

An original is priced based on what the market will bear for vintage amplifiers.

1959 Fender Bassman

This is another big boy. Like the Super, it has four 10" speakers and weighs around 53 pounds. I think this amp works best with the Astatic JT-30.

I have played through an original 1959 Fender Bassman that a store wanted $10,000.00 for! I ended up buying a reissue of this amp on E-Bay for a fraction of that amount. The sound is big, warm, and powerful. This is your basic Holy Grail amp for harp and guitar players.

Once again, this amplifier does not have reverb. I use the same digital delay mentioned previously.

Be careful not to go overboard when trying to electrify your sound. You want just enough overdrive to give you a warm, big sound with an edge; just don't go over that edge.

It's hard to go wrong using the right amps and mic. Remember to get advice on your tone from other musicians and harp players to dial in the right tone for your playing. Once again, each venue will sound different so be open to changing your settings depending on where you are playing.

It is time for our last YouTube demonstration. This one will demonstrate the sounds of several harp amplifiers. The video is entitled "Tim Gartland on Harp Amplifiers". You can search by title.

****SPOTLIGHT****

I mentioned my 1959 Fender Bassman reissue above. Fender has reissued a number of amps including my 1965 super Reverb because older amps just sound better.

Highlights:

If you are just starting out, there is a good sounding amplifier from Fender called the Blues Junior.

1965 Fender Super Reverb has four 10" inch speakers so it is very loud.

1962 Fender Princeton: This is small amp with a big sound. This amp has one 10" speaker.

1959 Fender Bassman is another big boy like the Super; it has four 10" speakers and a warm full tone.

The 1965 Super Reverb and the 1959 Bassman are being re-issued and are available at reasonable prices.

Demonstration (Track 31 on MP3's) :

➢ Demonstrate each amplifier

FAQ: If I buy the right mic and the right amplifier, will I become an instant harp legend?

Answer: The right equipment will point you in the right direction but you have to travel the rest of the way yourself. The fact is that your sound has more to do with how you play than what equipment you use.

Pictured are the 1965 Fender Super Reverb and Fender Blues Junior.

Chapter 32

The Art of Conversation: Playing Behind Singers and Soloists

"Support you local musician"

-bumper sticker

173

Playing in a band is about supporting each other as musicians in the pursuit of making great music

Once you can play well enough to make music with others, you will want to make sure you are invited back. Part of this is about being a complimentary player when you are not soloing. *Comping, as it is known, is playing in the background in a way that compliments the singer or other soloist.*

Comping

The Do's:

Understand playing in a band is a team sport.

Before choosing to comp, ask yourself "is what I am about to play going to make the song better?"

Being a good conversationalist is more about being a good listener than a good talker. It is the same thing with comping. Listen to your band mates and try to play something that helps their performance.

Make sure you are at an appropriate volume. This level is often well below your solo volume.

Be just as thoughtful about what you *do not* want to play as what you do want to play.

The Don'ts:

Don't try to steal the vocalist/soloists thunder. It is transparent to the audience and annoying to your fellow musicians.

Don't talk to other musicians or the audience while another musician is soloing or singing. Listen to what your band mate is trying to say.

Comping may be as simple as playing the note of the current chord of the song. Get a copy of the chords, or changes as they are referred to.

It can also be effective to answer the singer or soloist with what is known as a *fill*. *A fill is a space in the music where either the singer is not singing or the soloist is not playing.*

Highlights:

Understand playing in a band is a team sport.

Before choosing to Comp, ask yourself if what I am about to play is going to make the song better?

Make sure your level is below your solo volume.

It can also be effective to answer the singer or soloist with what is known as a *fill*.

Demonstration (Track 32 on MP3's) :

> ➢ Comping behind soloists
> ➢ Playing fills behind a vocalist

If you are interested in hearing more of my music, visit my website at timgartland.com or my YouTube channel.

Chapter 33

Begin by Asking:
Sitting In, Jams, and
Auditioning

"Music has to breathe and sweat. You have to play it live."

- James Brown

To get what you want, you have to work hard then you have to go out and get it. What is the point of learning to play if there isn't anybody to hear you? It's the proverbial "if the tree falls in the woods and nobody hears it, does it make a sound?" After all the hours of practicing, you eventually want someone other than your loved ones to hear you play!

Sitting in with bands

Before you ask, prepare for possible rejection and don't be offended. It's their call.

Wait until the band is on break before asking. Never ask in the middle of a set.

Prepare to audition on the spot. Several times I have been asked to play in the ear of the bandleader.

Make sure you have the right key harp for the song you are going to play with the band.

When the band calls you to the stage, you will want to hurry up to the stage. Don't hold up the show.

Listen and watch the front man to cue you regarding when to start and end your solo.

Open Mics and Jams

Most of these types of gigs have signup sheets to establish the order of when you will go up.

Take a bunch of harps with you. You never know what keys the songs will be in.

Have respect for the other musicians.

Have pen and paper with you. You may meet your future musical partner.

****SPOTLIGHT****

One of my favorite memories of jamming was Christmas Eve 1984. I had just moved to Chicago and was working at a record store. Being in retail I worked Christmas Eve day and was scheduled to work the day after Christmas. With everyone I knew and loved back in Ohio, I was on my own that Christmas.

The famous Kingston Mines blues club held its weekly Monday night blues jam despite the fact that it was Christmas Eve. After work that day I went down there to see if there would be anyone there to jam. I found out there were a lot of other people in similar situations. We ended up having a ball.

Auditioning for a Band

Be prepared. Try to get a recording of the band in advance and do your homework.

Joining a band is a lot like getting married so make sure you choose wisely.

Musicianship alone is not enough. Do you connect on a personal level?

Do you have the same musical aspirations?

Do you want to go on the road? How often do you plan on gigging?

How often does your significant other plan on you gigging?

Do you want to play original music versus covers?

What kind of money will you make?

Does the band want to record?

How often do they plan to rehearse?

Once again, give it some thought before committing.

Highlights:

Sitting In:
Prepare to get rejected and don't be offended. It is their call.

Open Mics and Jams:
Have pen and paper with you. You may meet your future musical partner

Auditioning for Bands:
Be prepared. Try to recordings in advance and do your homework

Demonstration (Track 33 on MP3's):

> ➢ Closing comments

> ****** SPOTLIGHT******
>
> *Thanks to my big brother Pat, the first concert I attended was a blues show. He knew I was messing around with the harp and would enjoy hearing the great Muddy Waters, Johnny Winter and James Cotton. That show sealed my musical fate. I wanted to play blues on the harp. My goal was to play with Muddy. Although I never reached that goal, as Muddy passed on April 30, 1983, I did play with the nucleus of his band that latter formed the Legendary Blues Band. This band included drummer Willie Smith, bassist Calvin Jones and piano immortal Pinetop Perkins. Many thanks go out to harp king Jerry Portnoy for letting me play that wonderful night.*

Performing with piano player extraordinaire, Tom West in Rockport,
Massachusetts.

Appendix:

All Notes in the 7 top Harp Keys and Harp Position Chart

This appendix is for you to use as a reference to all the notes possible on the diatonic harp through bending. There are 12 keys in music but I chose the 7 most popular keys for playing blues, folk, country and rock and roll. This can be used to figure out where the notes are for parts or solos to songs you are trying to learn.

A Harp

	1	2	3	4	5	6	7	8	9	10
Full Note Bend										G
Half Note Bend								C	D#	G#
Blow	A	C#	E	A	C#	E	A	C#	E	A
	1	2	3	4	5	6	7	8	9	10
Draw	B	E	G#	B	D	F#	G#	B	D	F#
Half Note Bend	A#	D#	G	A#	F					
Full Note Bend		D	F#							
Full and 1/2 Bend			F							

Bb Harp

	1	2	3	4	5	6	7	8	9	10
Full Note Bend										Ab
Half Note Bend								Db	E	A
Blow	Bb	D	F	Bb	D	F	Bb	D	F	Bb
	1	2	3	4	5	6	7	8	9	10
Draw	C	F	A	C	Eb	G	A	C	Eb	G
Half Note Bend	B	E	Ab	B		Gb				
Full Note Bend		Eb	G							
Full and 1/2 Bend			Gb							

C Harp

	1	2	3	4	5	6	7	8	9	10
Full Note Bend										A#
Half Note Bend								D#	F#	B
Blow	C	E	G	C	E	G	C	E	G	C
	1	2	3	4	5	6	7	8	9	10
Draw	D	G	B	D	F	A	B	D	F	A
Half Note Bend	C#	F#	A#	C#		G#				
Full Note Bend		F	A							
Full and 1/2 Bend			G#							

D Harp										
Full Note Bend										C
Half Note Bend								F	G#	C#
Blow	D	F#	A	D	F#	A	D	F#	A	D
	1	2	3	4	5	6	7	8	9	10
Draw	E	A	C#	E	G	B	C#	E	G	B
Half Note Bend	D#	G#	C	D#		A#				
Full Note Bend		G	B							
Full and 1/2 Bend			A#							

Eb Harp										
Full Note Bend										Db
Half Note Bend								Gb	A	D
Blow	Eb	G	Bb	Eb	G	Bb	Eb	G	Bb	Eb
	1	2	3	4	5	6	7	8	9	10
Draw	F	Bb	D	F	Ab	C	D	F	Ab	C
Half Note Bend	E	A	Db	E		B				
Full Note Bend		Ab	C							
Full and 1/2 Bend			B							

F Harp										
Full Note Bend										D#
Half Note Bend								G#	B	E
Blow	F	A	C	F	A	C	F	A	C	F
	1	2	3	4	5	6	7	8	9	10
Draw	G	C	E	G	A#	D	E	G	A#	D
Half Note Bend	F#	B	D#	F#		C#				
Full Note Bend		A#	D							
Full and 1/2 Bend			C#							

G Harp										
Full Note Bend										F
Half Note Bend								A#	C#	F#
Blow	G	B	D	G	B	D	G	B	D	G
	1	2	3	4	5	6	7	8	9	10
Draw	A	D	F#	A	C	E	F#	A	C	E
Half Note Bend	G#	C#	F	G#		D#				
Full Note Bend		C	E							
Full and 1/2 Bend			D#							

185

The chart below indicates what key harmonica you would use for all three positions based on the key the song is in.

If the song Key is:	First Position Harmonica Key	Second Position Harmonica Key:	Third Position Harmonica Key:
A	A	D	G
B flat	B flat	E Flat	A Flat
C	C	F	B Flat
D	D	G	C
E	E	A	D
F	F	B Flat	E Flat
G	G	C	F

Here are the root notes for the I, IV and V chords in all three positions.

Position	Holes 1 to 4	Holes 4 to 8	Holes 7 to 10
First	1+, 2full, 2	4+, 5, 6+	7+, 9, 9+
Second	2, 4+, 4	6+, 7+, 8	
Third	1, 2, 3full	4, 6+, 6	8, 9+, 10

Made in the USA
Monee, IL
25 February 2021